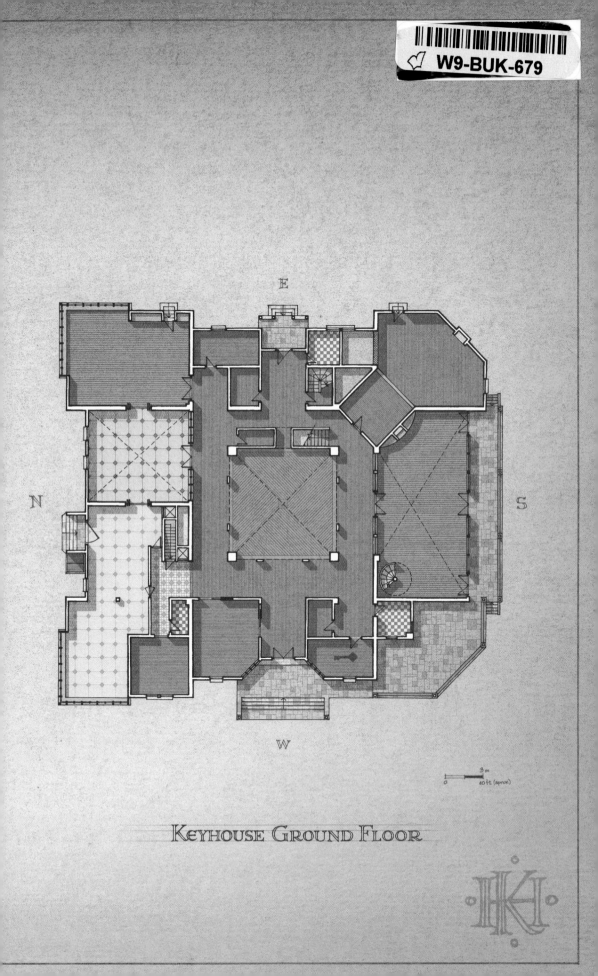

E

N

S

W

3 m

0   10 ft (aprox.)

Keyhouse Ground Floor

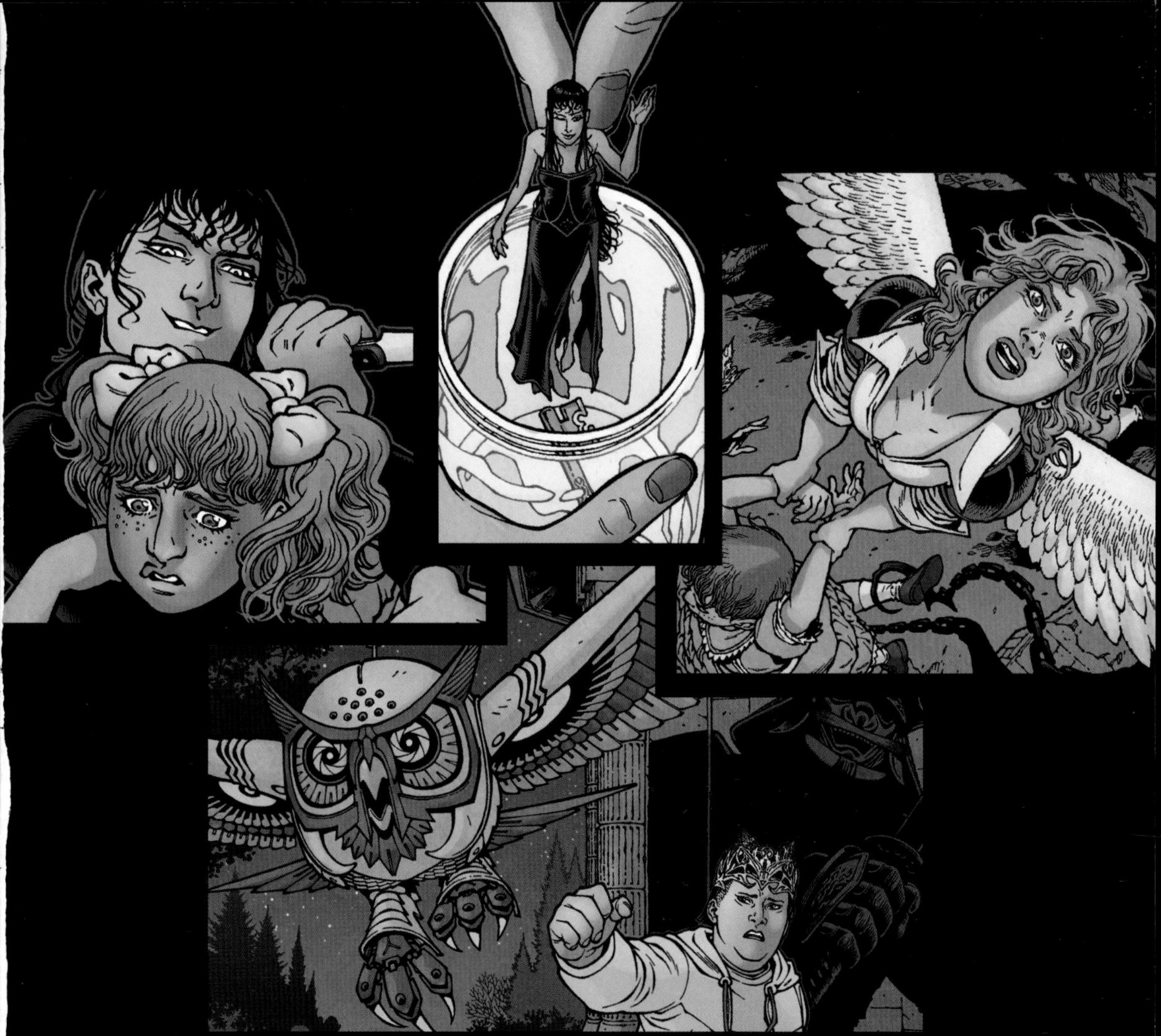

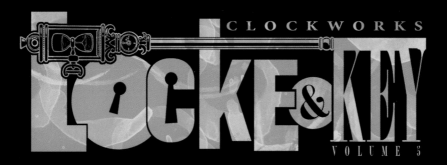

LOCKE & KEY

CLOCKWORKS

VOLUME 5

WRITTEN BY

JOE HILL

ART BY

GABRIEL RODRIGUEZ

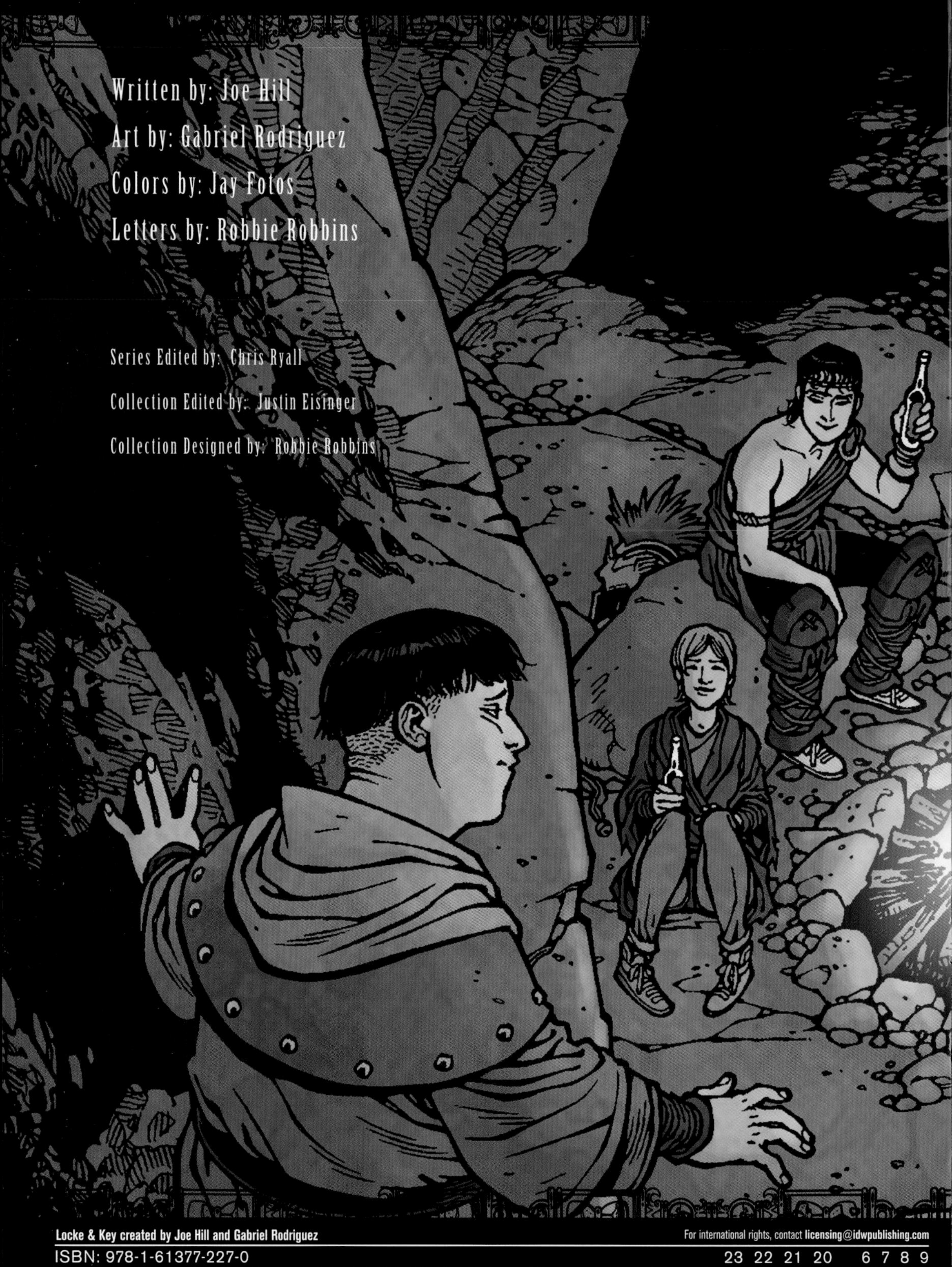

Written by: Joe Hill

Art by: Gabriel Rodriguez

Colors by: Jay Fotos

Letters by: Robbie Robbins

Series Edited by: Chris Ryall

Collection Edited by: Justin Eisinger

Collection Designed by: Robbie Robbins

Locke & Key created by Joe Hill and Gabriel Rodriguez

For international rights, contact licensing@idwpublishing.com

ISBN: 978-1-61377-227-0

23 22 21 20   6 7 8 9

www.IDWPUBLISHING.com

Chris Ryall, President & Publisher/CCO • Cara Morrison, Chief Financial Officer • Matthew Ruzicka, Chief Accounting Officer • David Hedgecock, Associate Publisher • John Barber, Editor-in-Chief • Justin Eisinger, Editorial Director, Graphic Novels and Collections • Jerry Bennington, VP of New Product Development • Lorelei Bunjes, VP of Technology & Information Services • Jud Meyers, Sales Director • Anna Morrow, Marketing Director • Tara McCrillis, Director of Design & Production • Mike Ford, Director of Operations • Rebekah Cahalin, General Manager

Ted Adams and Robbie Robbins, IDW Founders

Facebook: facebook.com/idwpublishing • Twitter: @idwpublishing • YouTube: youtube.com/idwpublishing
Tumblr: tumblr.idwpublishing.com • Instagram: instagram.com/idwpublishing

LOCKE & KEY, VOL. 5: CLOCKWORKS. JANUARY 2020. SIXTH PRINTING. Locke & Key script © 2020 Joe Hill, art © 2020 Idea and Design Works, LLC. All Rights Reserved. IDW Publishing, a division of Idea and Design Works, LLC. Editorial offices: 2765 Truxtun Road, San Diego, CA 92106. The IDW logo is registered in the U.S. Patent and Trademark Office. Any similarities to persons living or dead are purely coincidental. With the exception of artwork used for review purposes, none of the contents of this publication may be reprinted without the permission of Idea and Design Works, LLC. Printed in Korea.
IDW Publishing does not read or accept unsolicited submissions of ideas, stories, or artwork.
Originally published as LOCKE & KEY: CLOCKWORKS Issues #1–6.

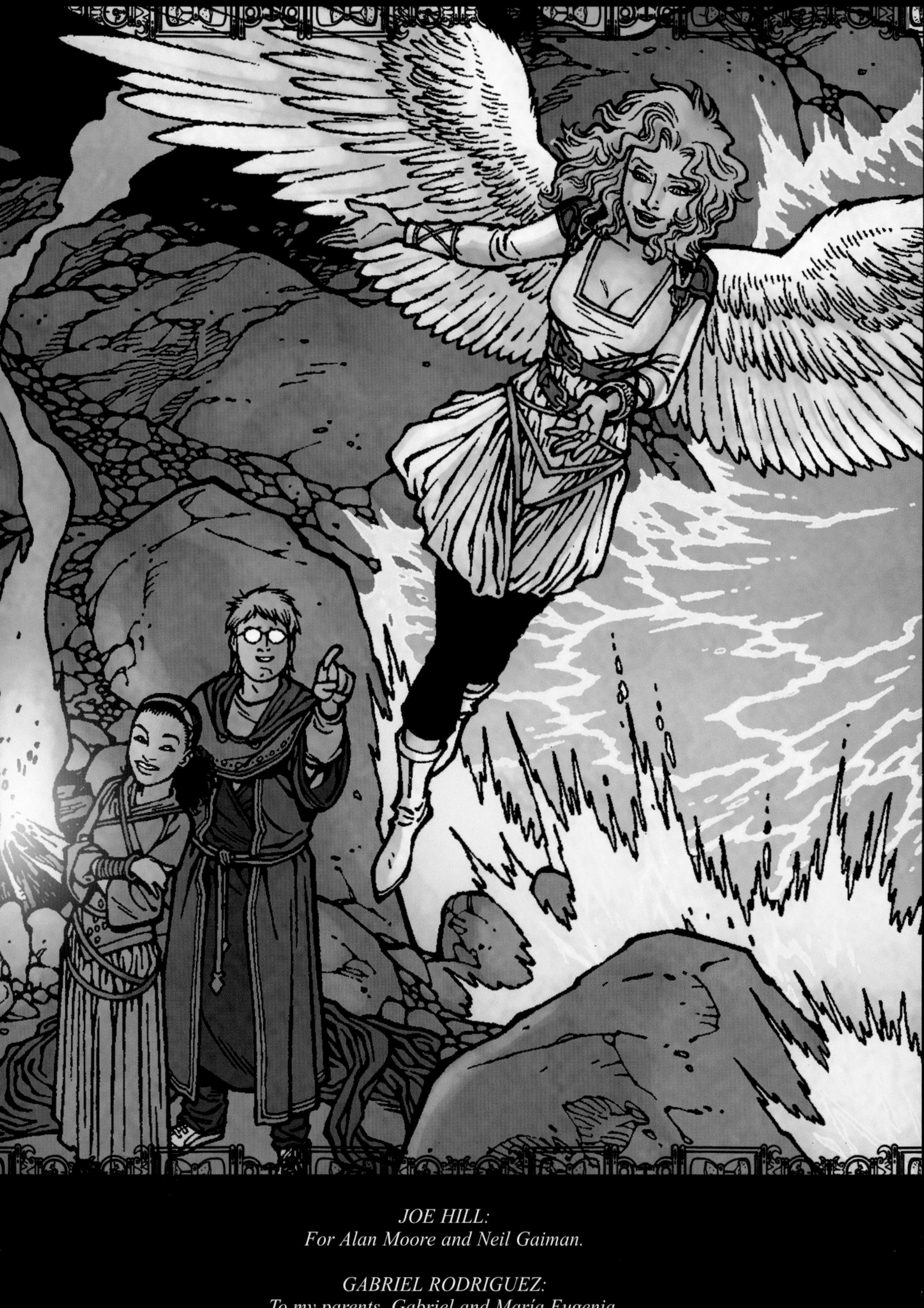

JOE HILL:
For Alan Moore and Neil Gaiman.

GABRIEL RODRIGUEZ:
To my parents, Gabriel and María Eugenia,
with love and gratitude.

-CLOCKWORKS-

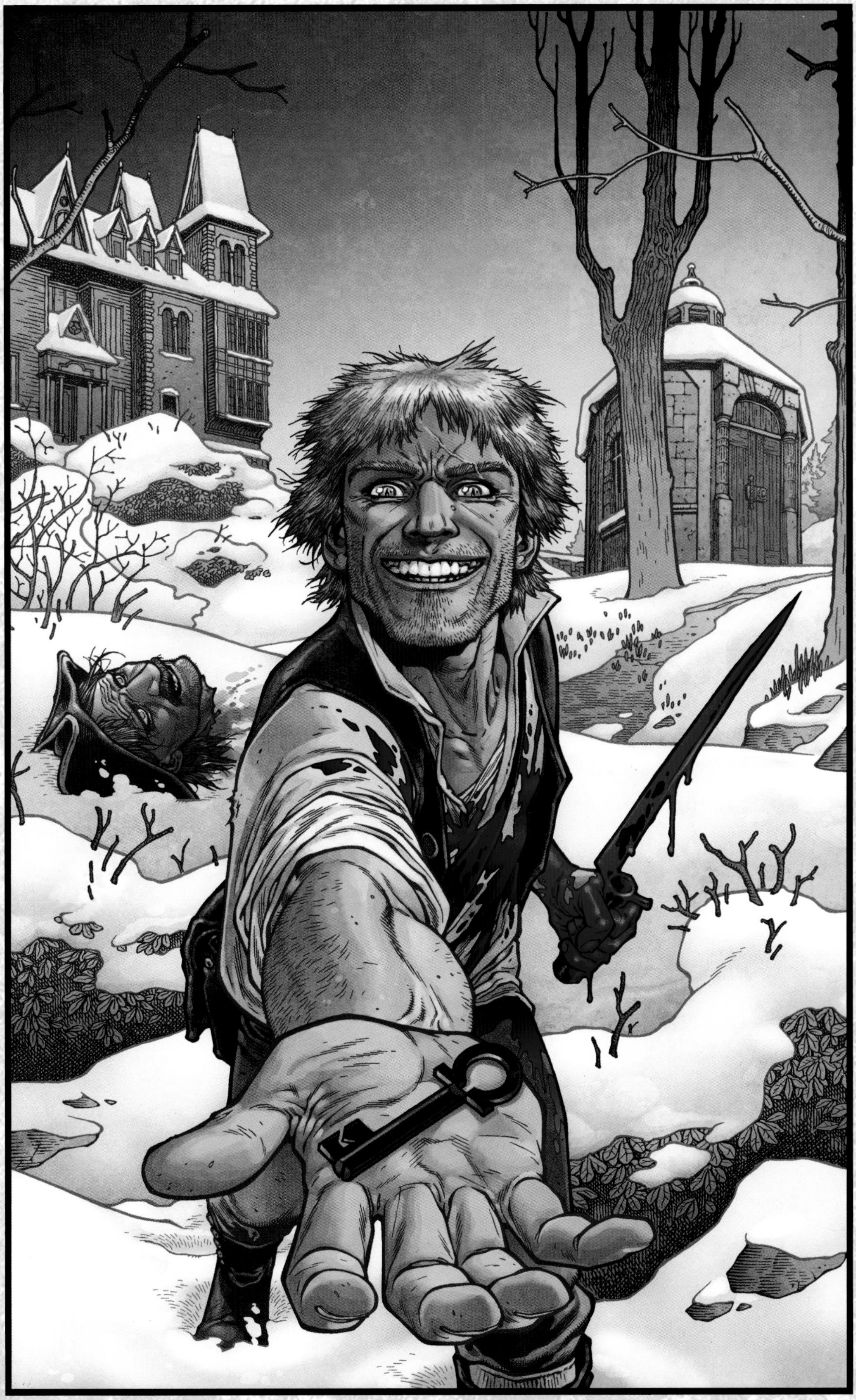

- CLOCKWORKS -

Chapter One

THE LOCKSMITH'S SON

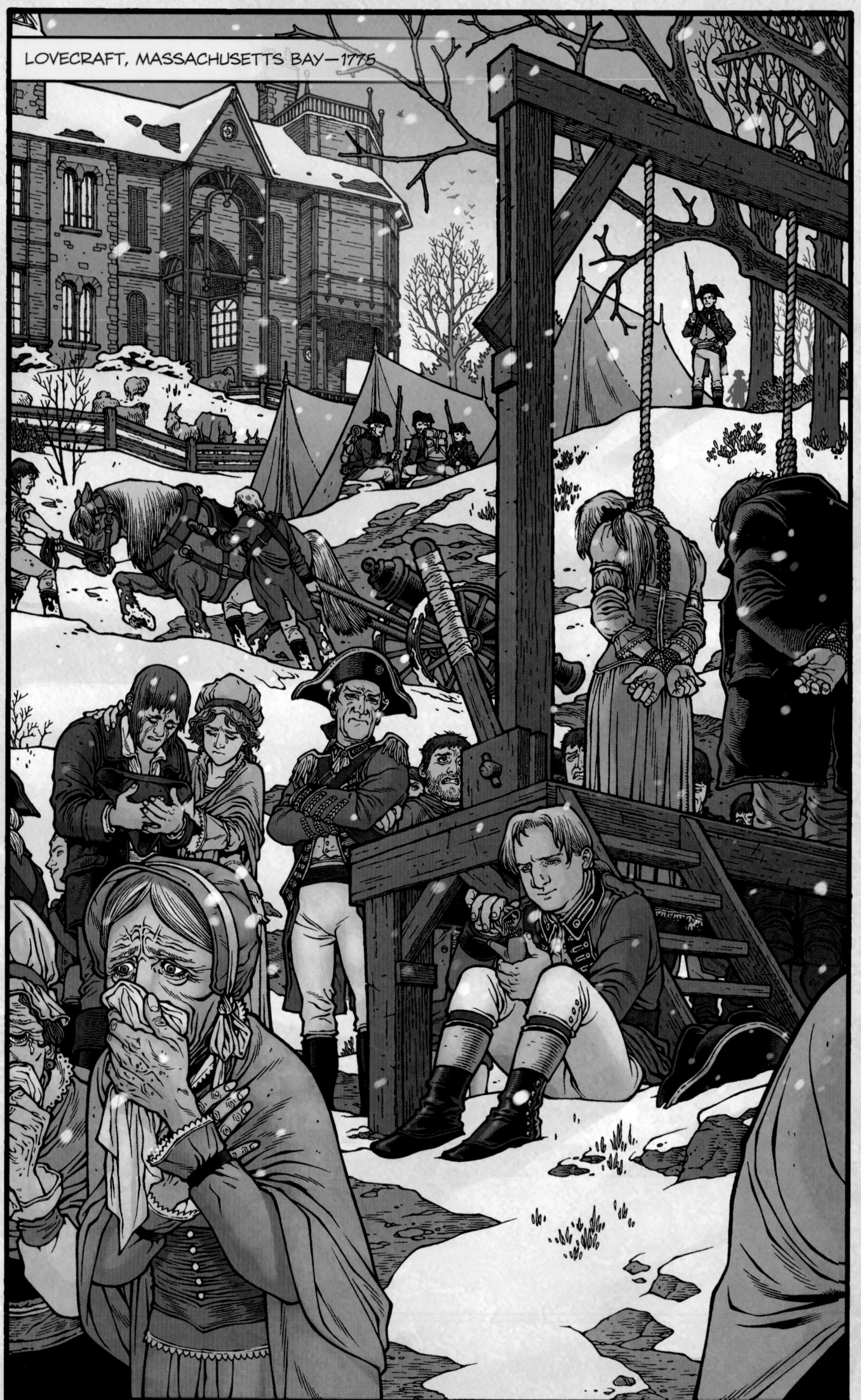
LOVECRAFT, MASSACHUSETTS BAY—1775

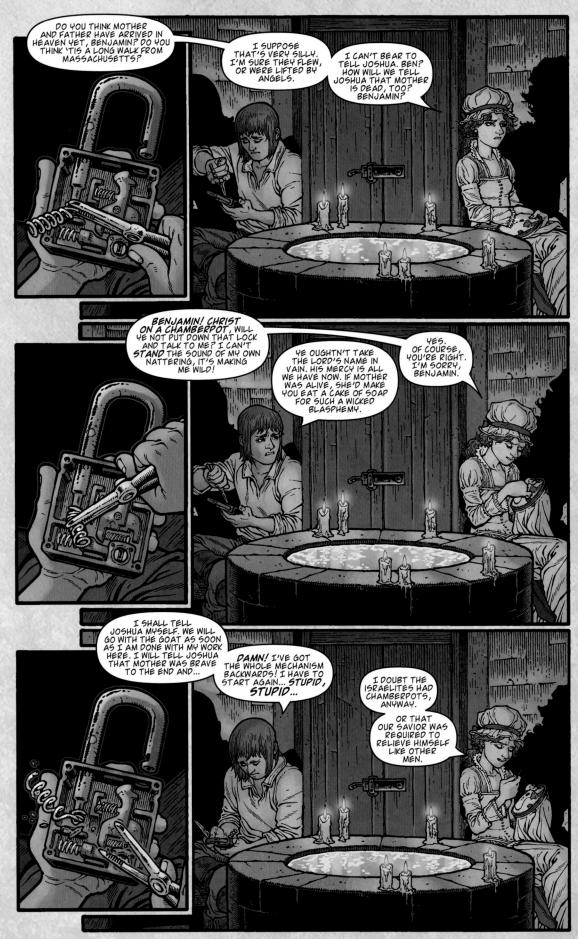

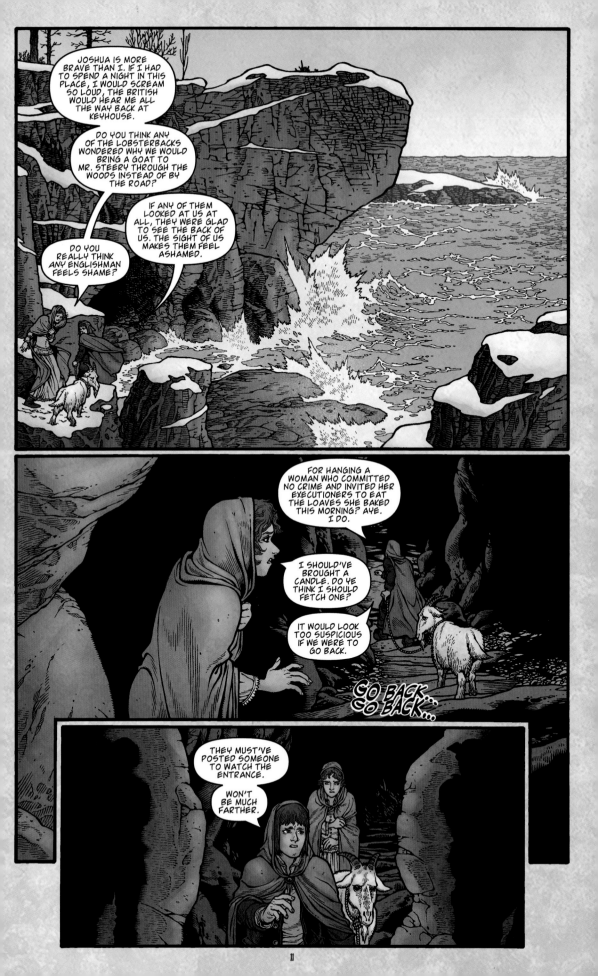

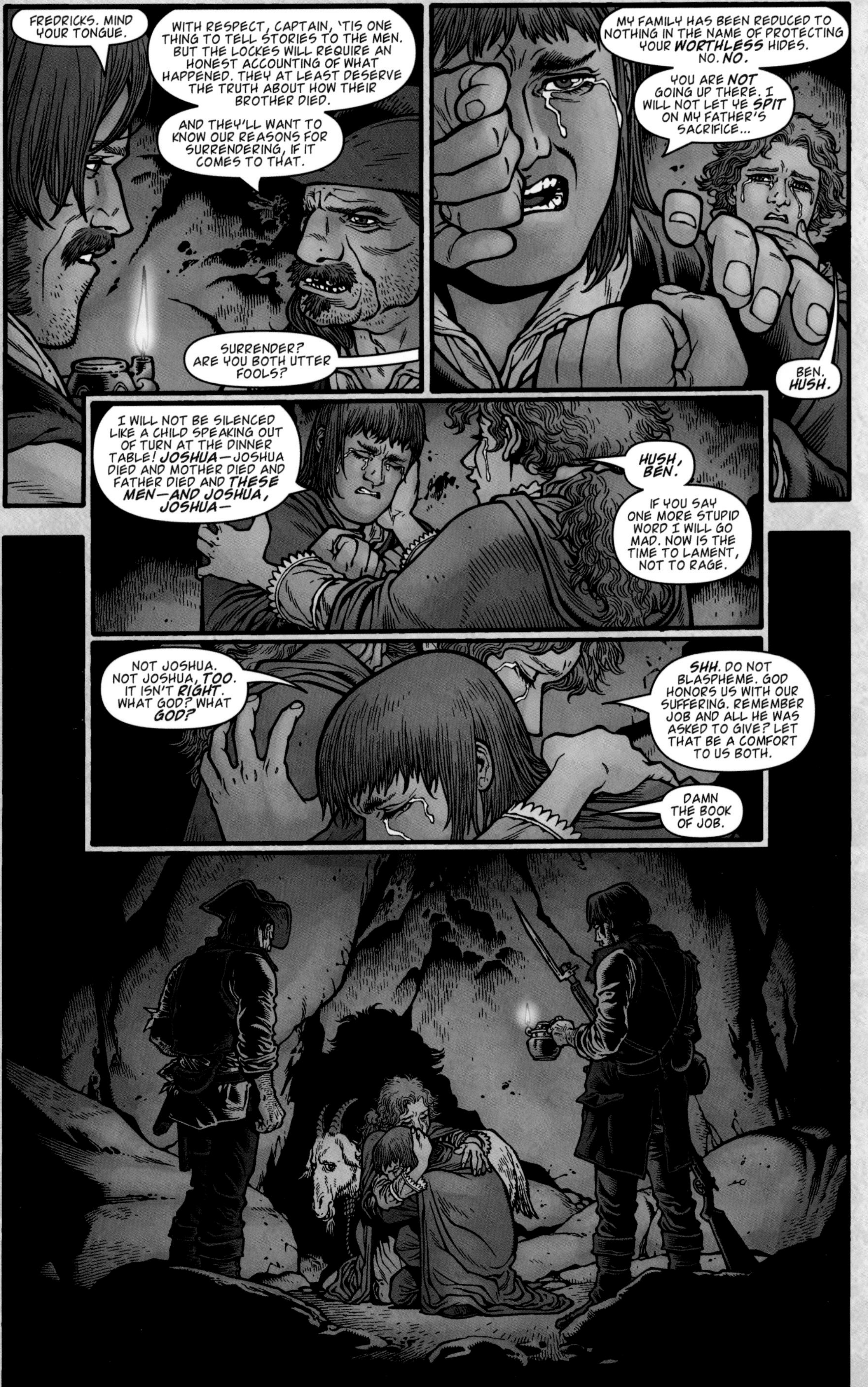
FREDRICKS. MIND YOUR TONGUE.
WITH RESPECT, CAPTAIN, 'TIS ONE THING TO TELL STORIES TO THE MEN. BUT THE LOCKES WILL REQUIRE AN HONEST ACCOUNTING OF WHAT HAPPENED. THEY AT LEAST DESERVE THE TRUTH ABOUT HOW THEIR BROTHER DIED.
AND THEY'LL WANT TO KNOW OUR REASONS FOR SURRENDERING, IF IT COMES TO THAT.
SURRENDER? ARE YOU BOTH UTTER FOOLS?
MY FAMILY HAS BEEN REDUCED TO NOTHING IN THE NAME OF PROTECTING YOUR WORTHLESS HIDES. NO. NO.
YOU ARE NOT GOING UP THERE. I WILL NOT LET YE SPIT ON MY FATHER'S SACRIFICE...
BEN. HUSH.
I WILL NOT BE SILENCED LIKE A CHILD SPEAKING OUT OF TURN AT THE DINNER TABLE! JOSHUA—JOSHUA DIED AND MOTHER DIED AND FATHER DIED AND THESE MEN—AND JOSHUA, JOSHUA—
HUSH, BEN.
IF YOU SAY ONE MORE STUPID WORD I WILL GO MAD. NOW IS THE TIME TO LAMENT, NOT TO RAGE.
NOT JOSHUA. NOT JOSHUA, TOO. IT ISN'T RIGHT. WHAT GOD? WHAT GOD?
SHH. DO NOT BLASPHEME. GOD HONORS US WITH OUR SUFFERING. REMEMBER JOB AND ALL HE WAS ASKED TO GIVE? LET THAT BE A COMFORT TO US BOTH.
DAMN THE BOOK OF JOB.

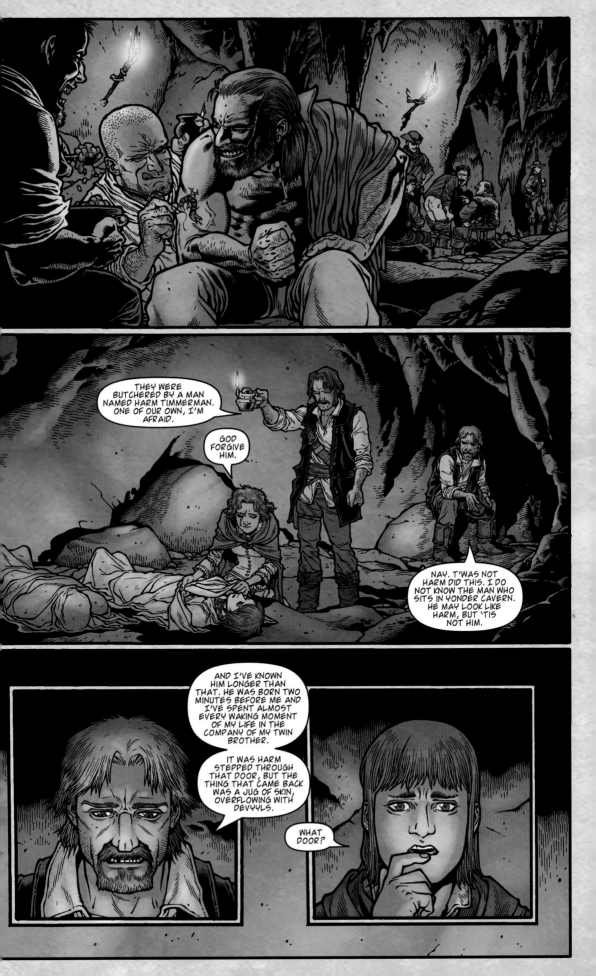

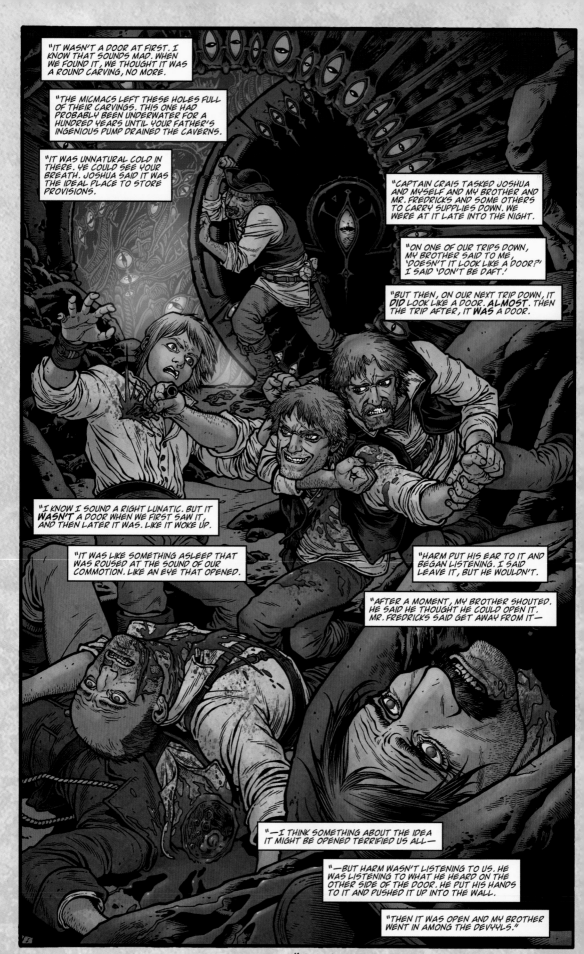

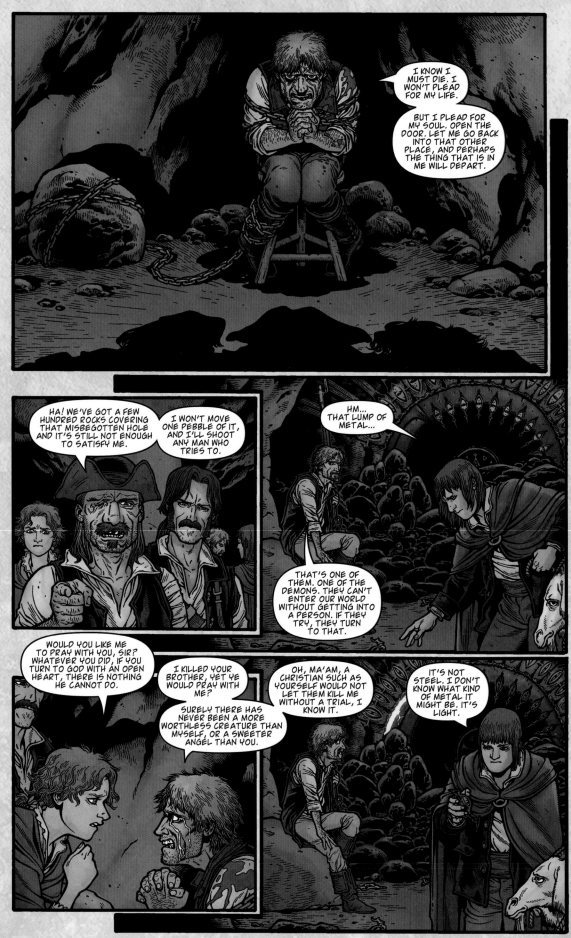

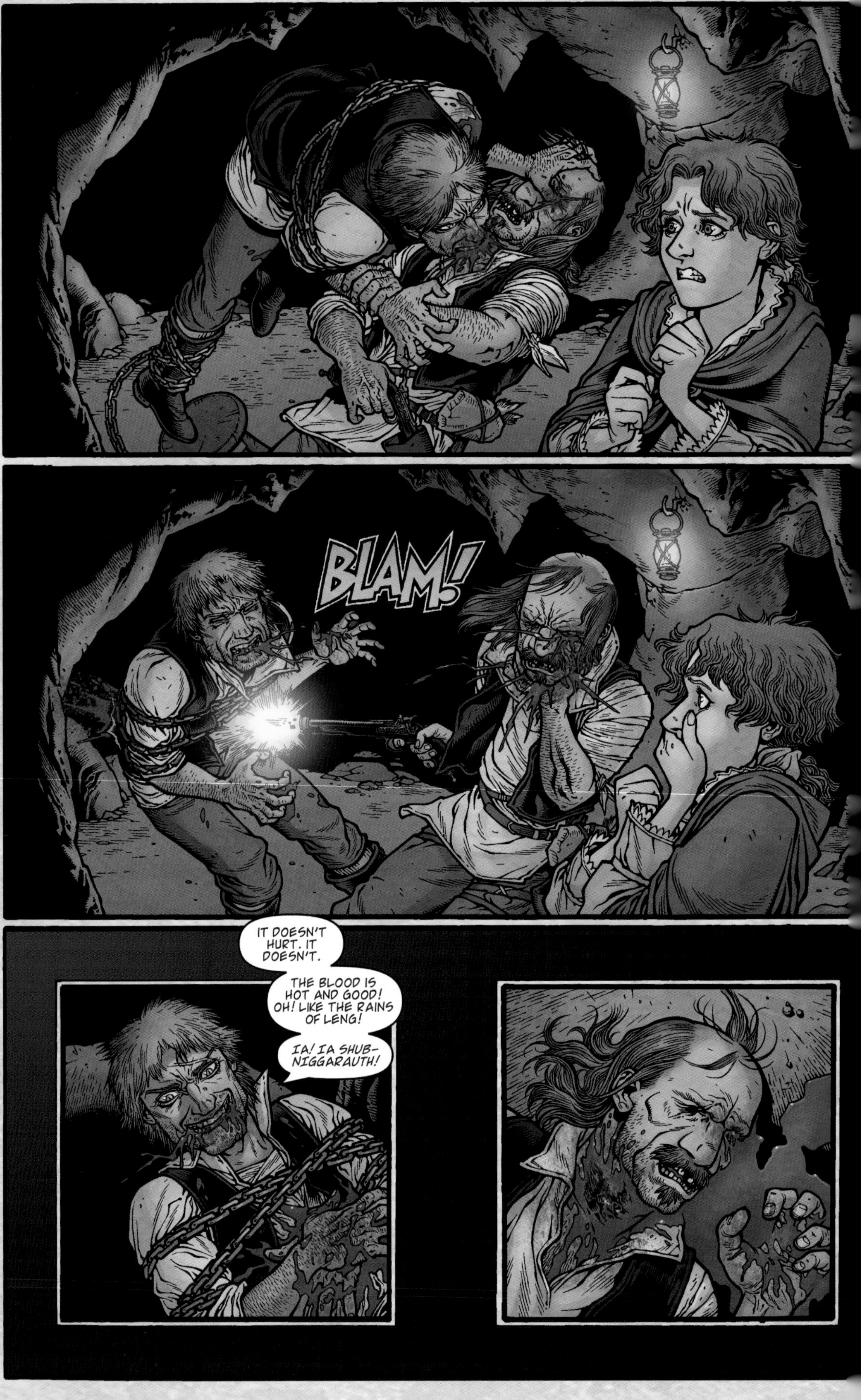
BLAM!
IT DOESN'T HURT. IT DOESN'T.
THE BLOOD IS HOT AND GOOD! OH! LIKE THE RAINS OF LENG!
IA! IA SHUB-NIGGARAUTH!

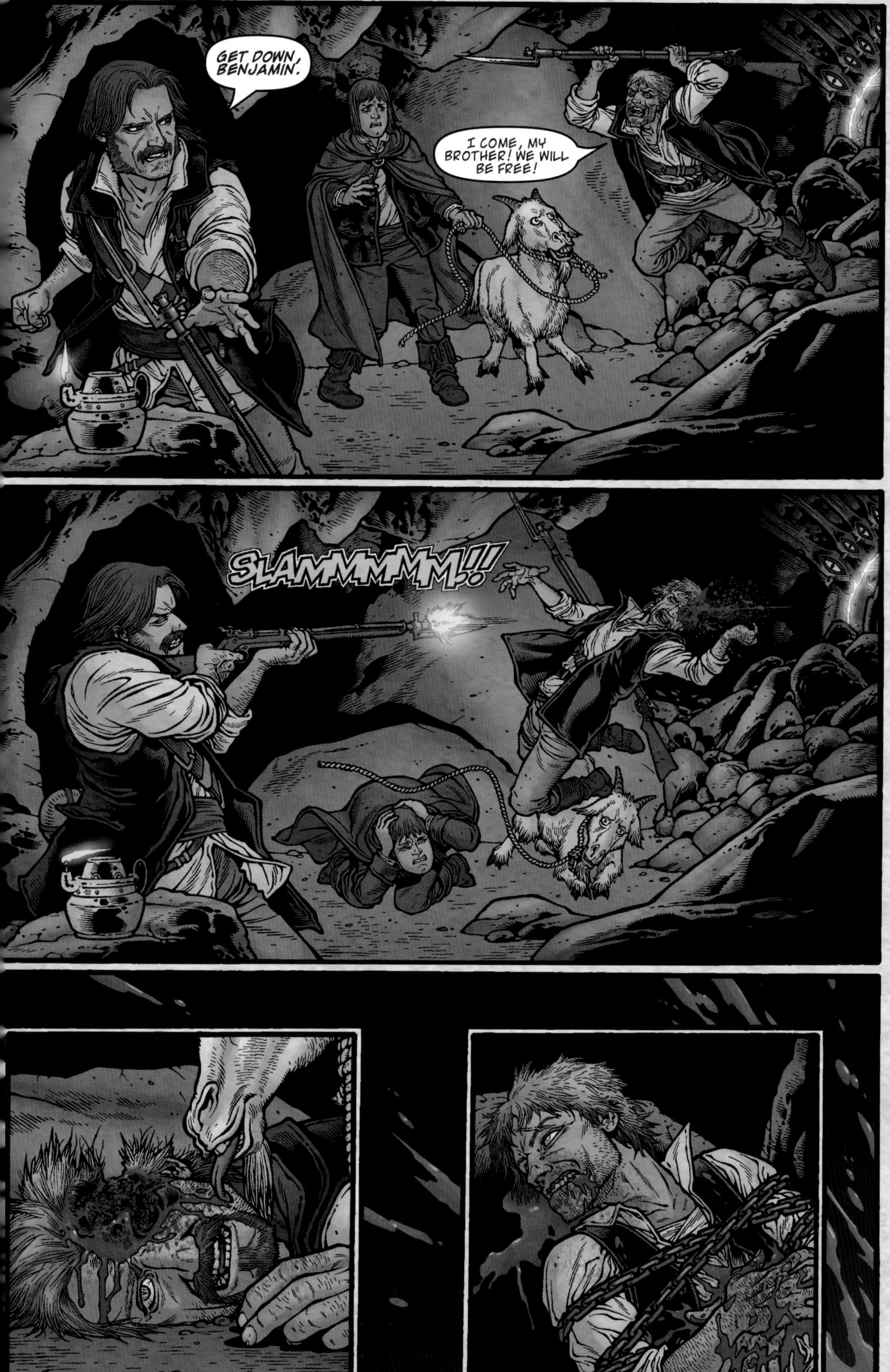
GET DOWN, BENJAMIN.
I COME, MY BROTHER! WE WILL BE FREE!
SLAMMMMMM!!

23

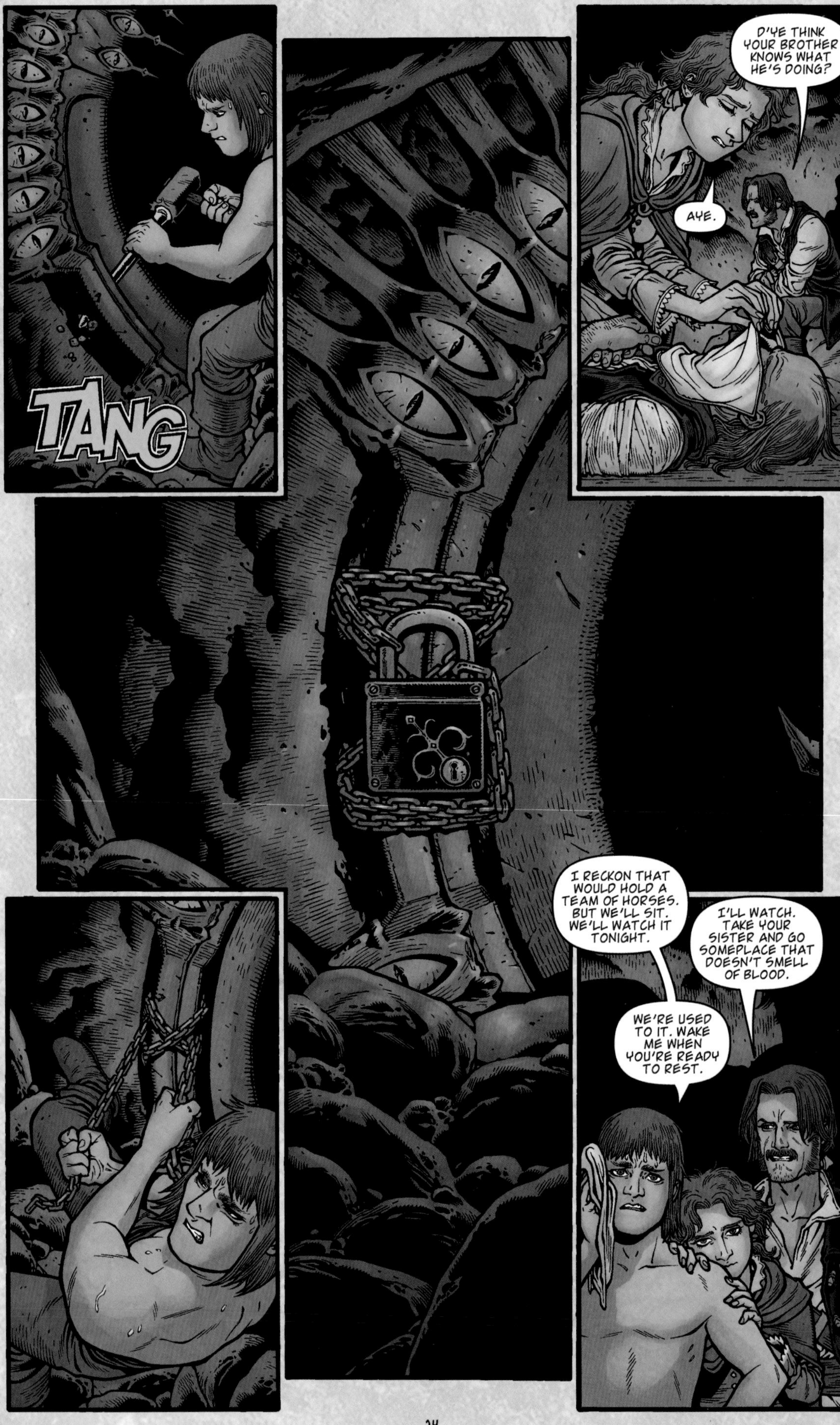
TANG
D'YE THINK YOUR BROTHER KNOWS WHAT HE'S DOING?
AYE.
I RECKON THAT WOULD HOLD A TEAM OF HORSES. BUT WE'LL SIT. WE'LL WATCH IT TONIGHT.
I'LL WATCH. TAKE YOUR SISTER AND GO SOMEPLACE THAT DOESN'T SMELL OF BLOOD.
WE'RE USED TO IT. WAKE ME WHEN YOU'RE READY TO REST.

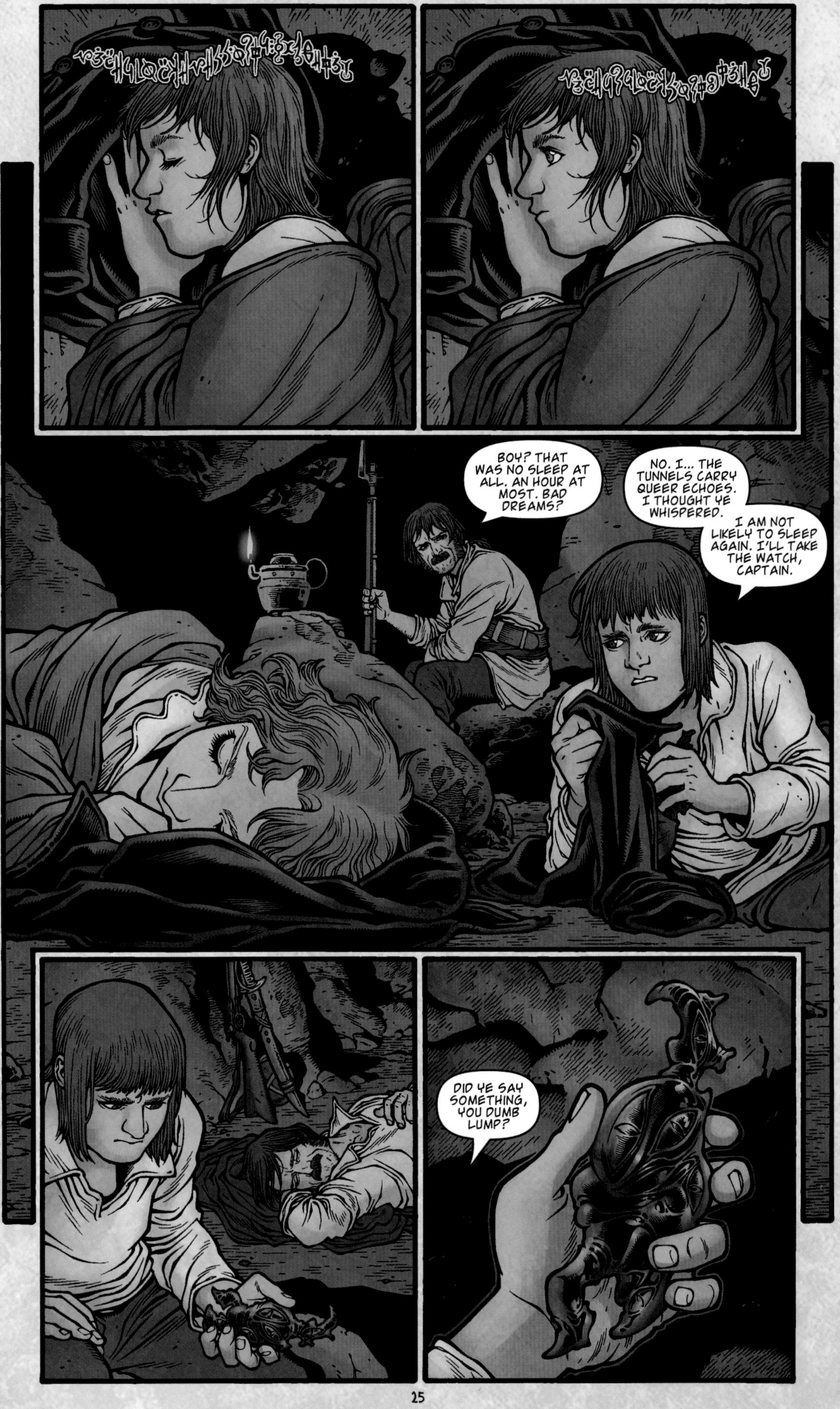
BOY? THAT WAS NO SLEEP AT ALL. AN HOUR AT MOST. BAD DREAMS?
NO. I... THE TUNNELS CARRY QUEER ECHOES. I THOUGHT YE WHISPERED.
I AM NOT LIKELY TO SLEEP AGAIN. I'LL TAKE THE WATCH, CAPTAIN.
DID YE SAY SOMETHING, YOU DUMB LUMP?

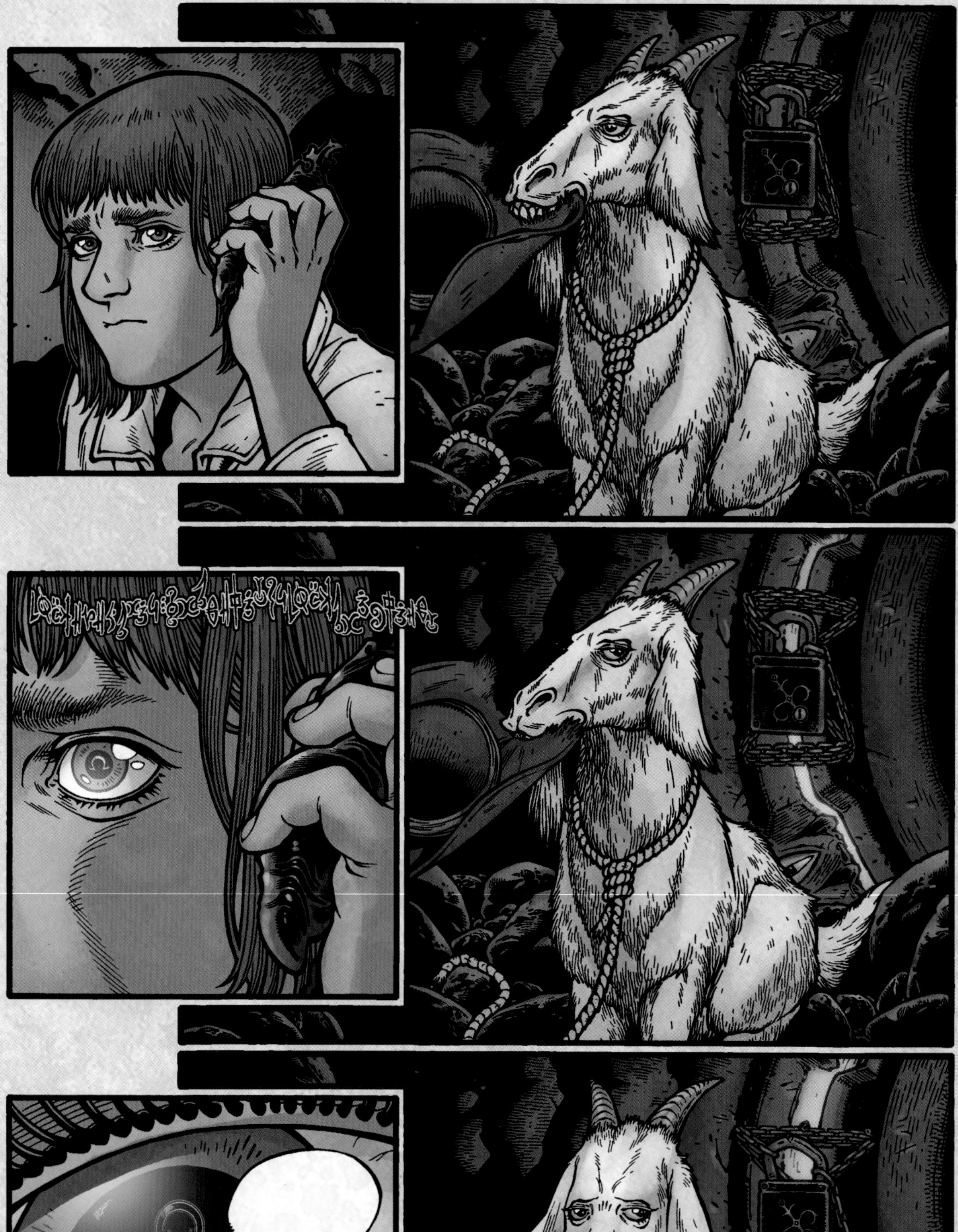

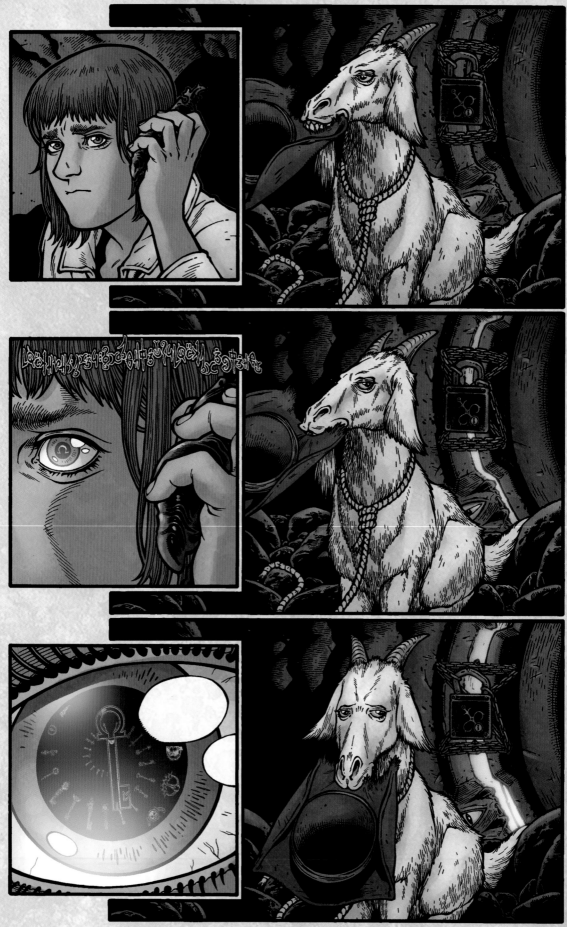

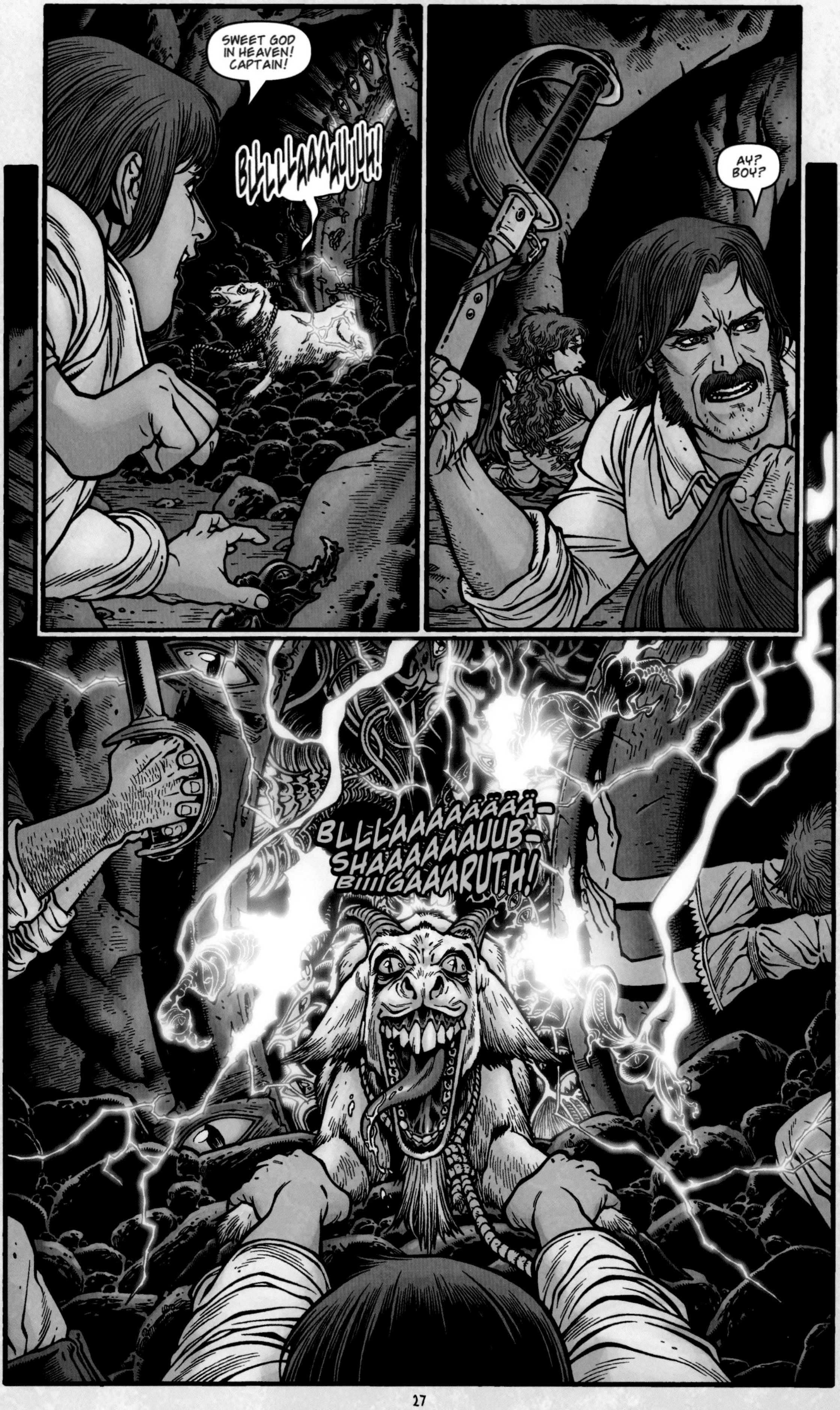
SWEET GOD IN HEAVEN! CAPTAIN!
BLLLLAAAAUUUH!
AY? BOY?
BLLLAAAAAAAÄ-
SHAAAAAAAUUB-
BIIIIGAAAARUTH!

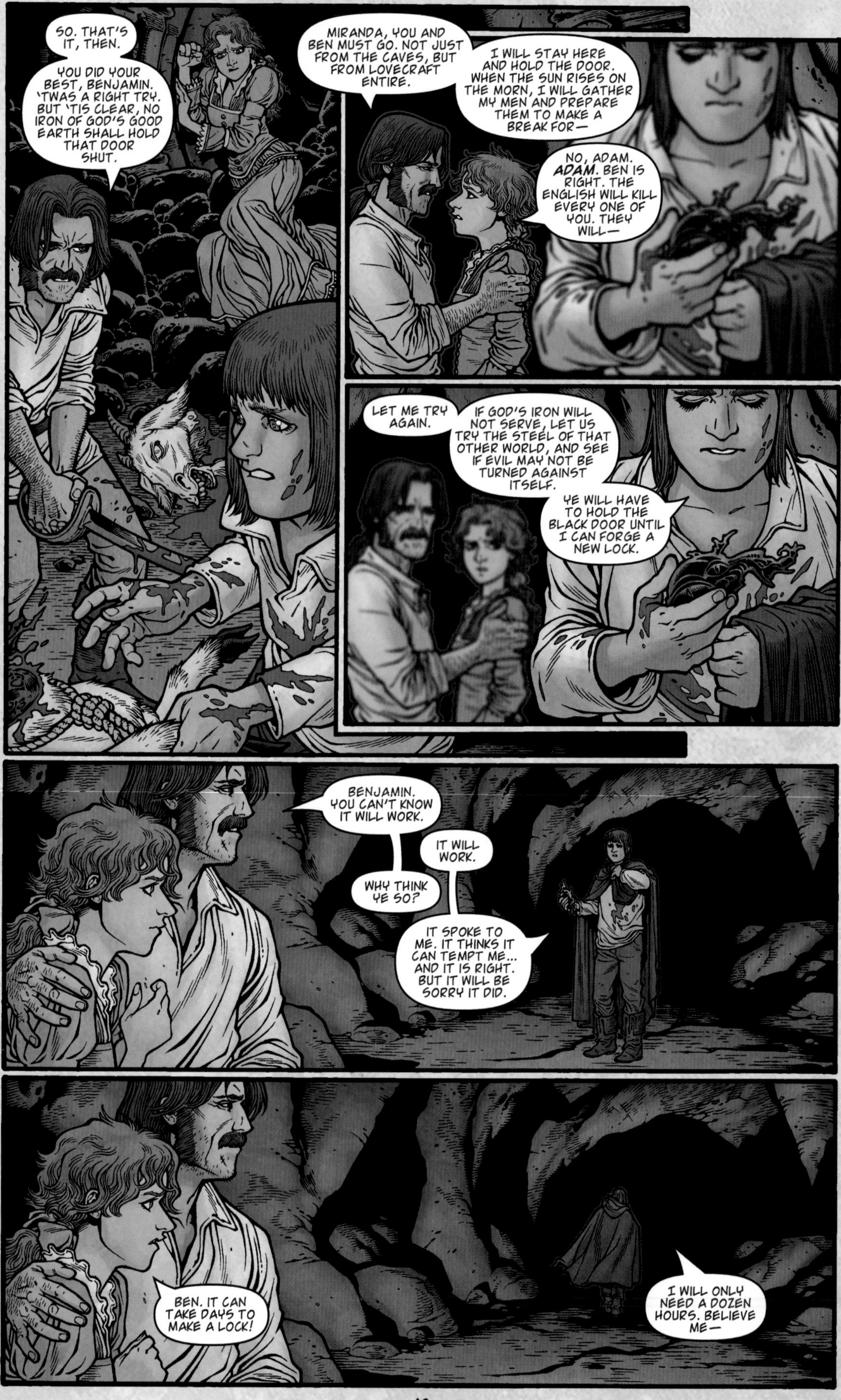
SO. THAT'S IT, THEN.
YOU DID YOUR BEST, BENJAMIN. 'TWAS A RIGHT TRY. BUT 'TIS CLEAR, NO IRON OF GOD'S GOOD EARTH SHALL HOLD THAT DOOR SHUT.
MIRANDA, YOU AND BEN MUST GO. NOT JUST FROM THE CAVES, BUT FROM LOVECRAFT ENTIRE.
I WILL STAY HERE AND HOLD THE DOOR. WHEN THE SUN RISES ON THE MORN, I WILL GATHER MY MEN AND PREPARE THEM TO MAKE A BREAK FOR—
NO, ADAM. ADAM. BEN IS RIGHT. THE ENGLISH WILL KILL EVERY ONE OF YOU. THEY WILL—
LET ME TRY AGAIN.
IF GOD'S IRON WILL NOT SERVE, LET US TRY THE STEEL OF THAT OTHER WORLD, AND SEE IF EVIL MAY NOT BE TURNED AGAINST ITSELF.
YE WILL HAVE TO HOLD THE BLACK DOOR UNTIL I CAN FORGE A NEW LOCK.
BENJAMIN. YOU CAN'T KNOW IT WILL WORK.
IT WILL WORK.
WHY THINK YE SO?
IT SPOKE TO ME. IT THINKS IT CAN TEMPT ME... AND IT IS RIGHT. BUT IT WILL BE SORRY IT DID.
BEN. IT CAN TAKE DAYS TO MAKE A LOCK!
I WILL ONLY NEED A DOZEN HOURS. BELIEVE ME—

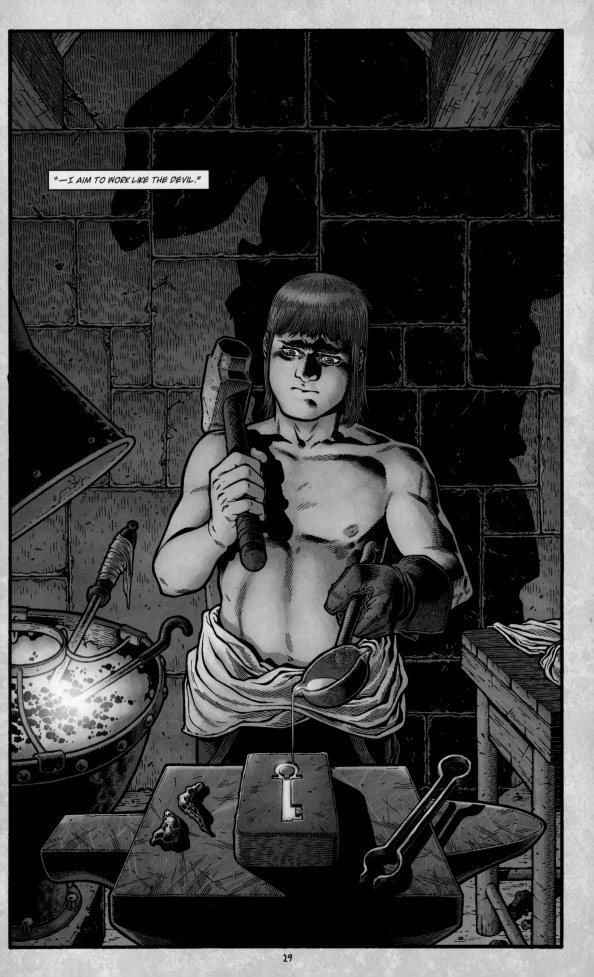

"—I AIM TO WORK LIKE THE DEVIL."

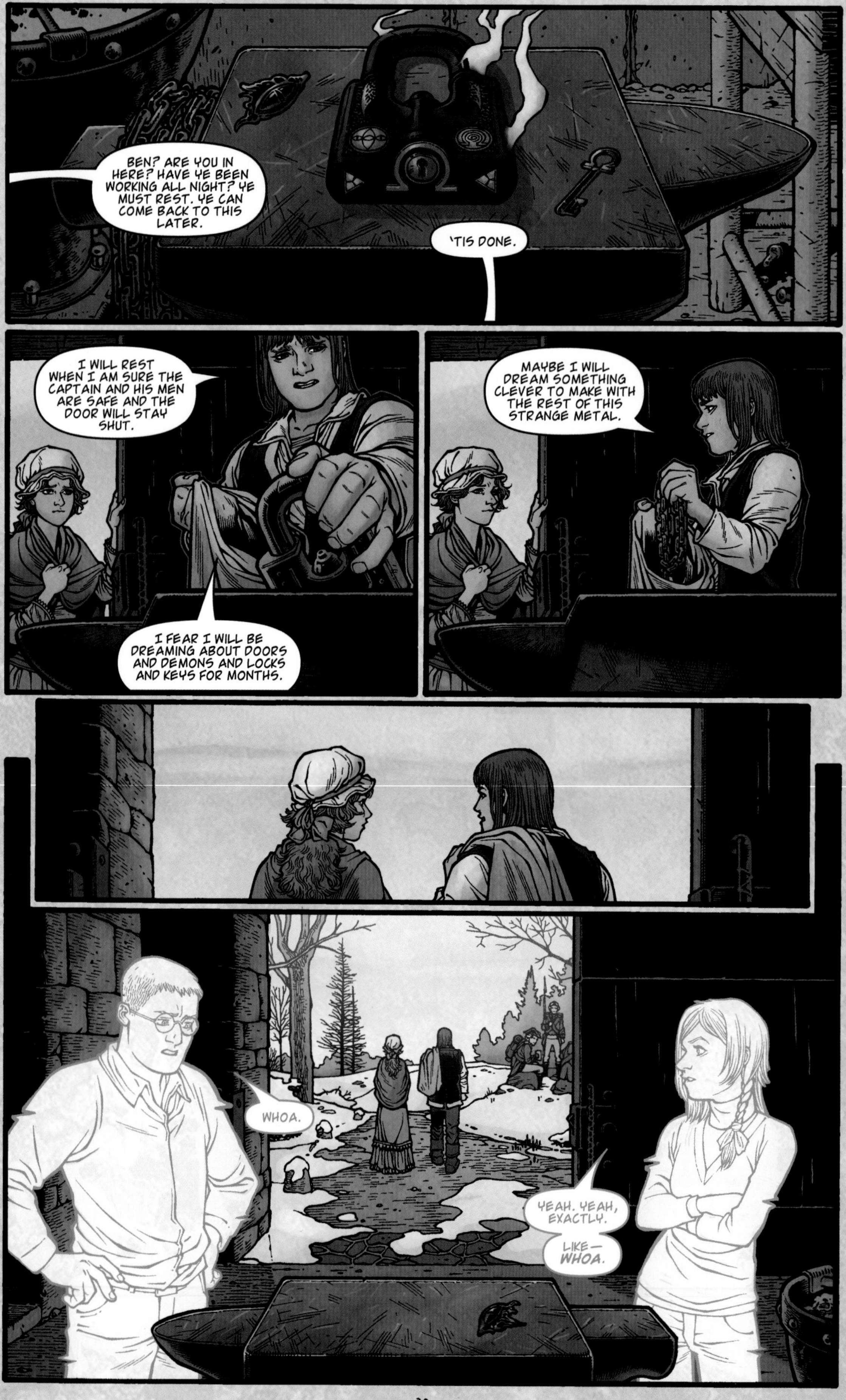
BEN? ARE YOU IN HERE? HAVE YE BEEN WORKING ALL NIGHT? YE MUST REST. YE CAN COME BACK TO THIS LATER.
'TIS DONE.
I WILL REST WHEN I AM SURE THE CAPTAIN AND HIS MEN ARE SAFE AND THE DOOR WILL STAY SHUT.
I FEAR I WILL BE DREAMING ABOUT DOORS AND DEMONS AND LOCKS AND KEYS FOR MONTHS.
MAYBE I WILL DREAM SOMETHING CLEVER TO MAKE WITH THE REST OF THIS STRANGE METAL.
WHOA.
YEAH. YEAH, EXACTLY.
LIKE— WHOA.

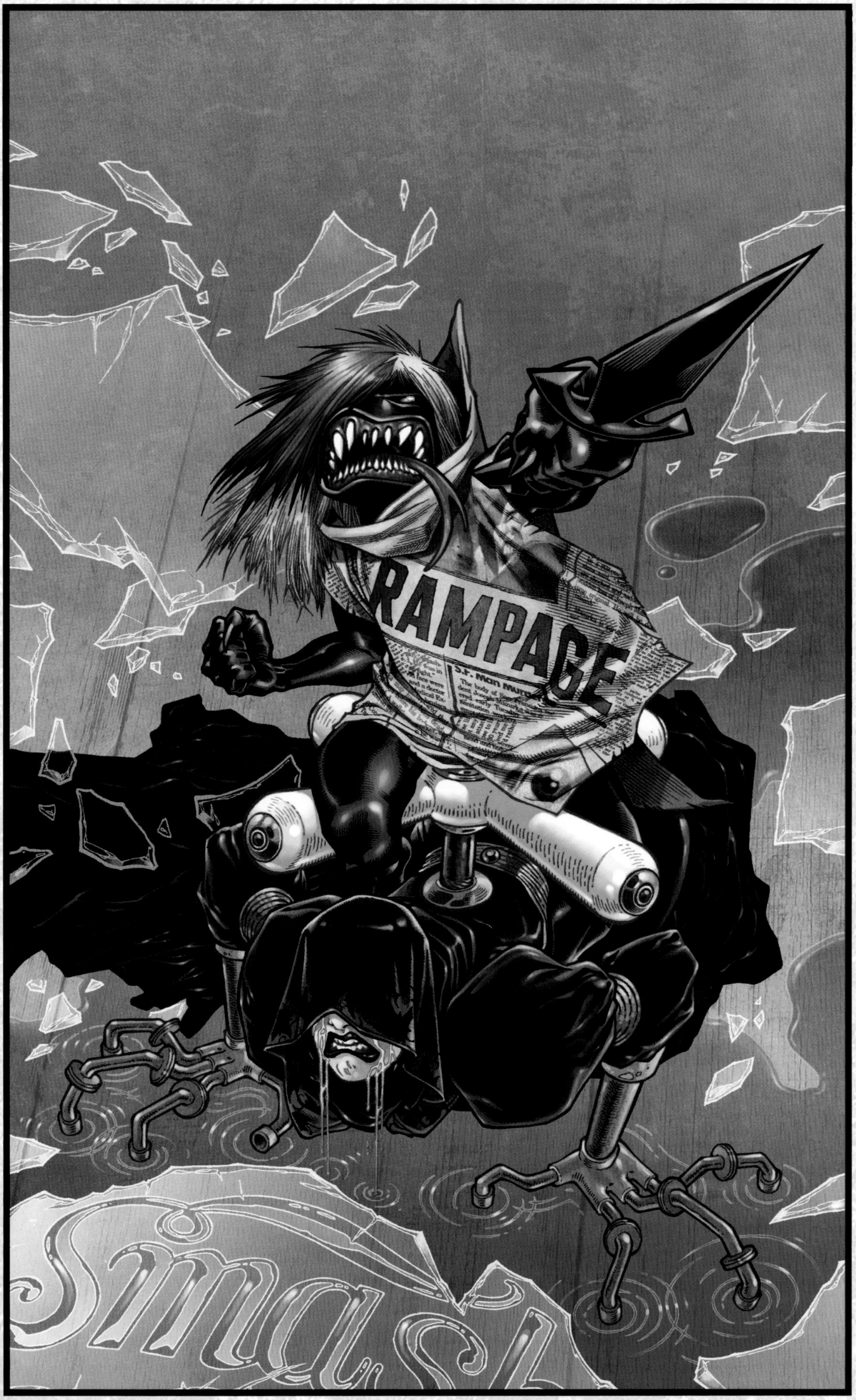
RAMPAGE

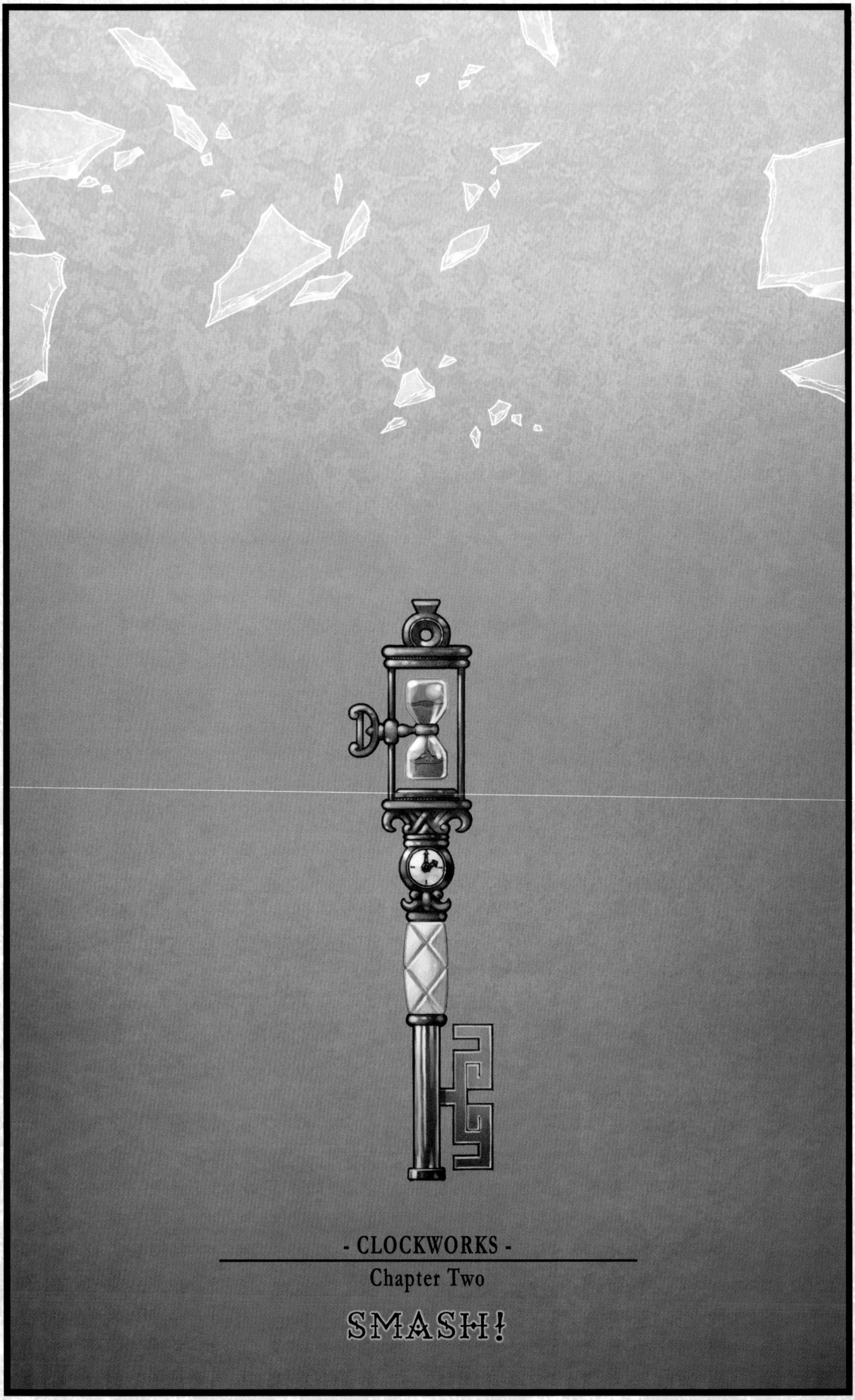

- CLOCKWORKS -

Chapter Two

SMASH!

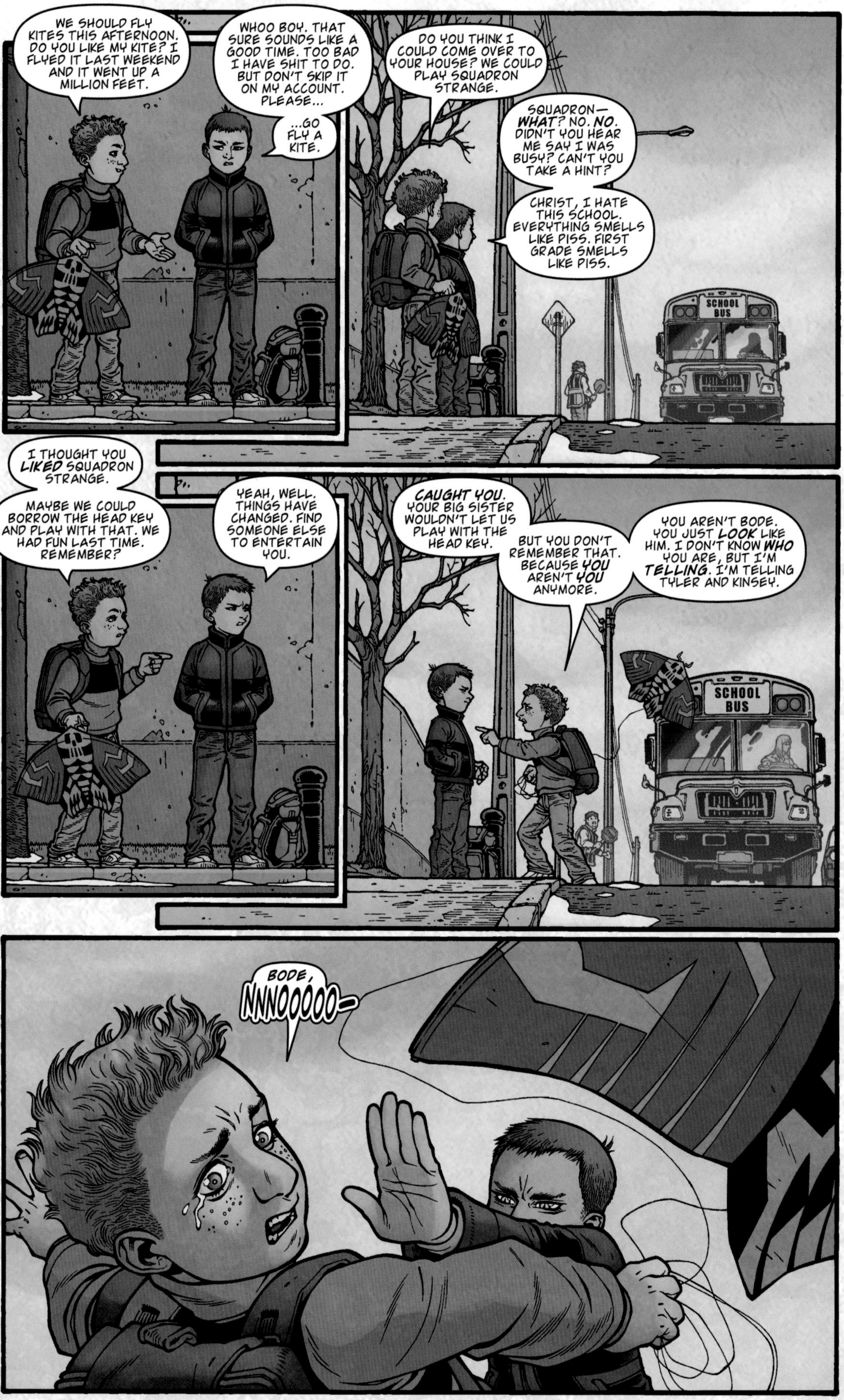

WE SHOULD FLY KITES THIS AFTERNOON. DO YOU LIKE MY KITE? I FLYED IT LAST WEEKEND AND IT WENT UP A MILLION FEET.
WHOO BOY. THAT SURE SOUNDS LIKE A GOOD TIME. TOO BAD I HAVE SHIT TO DO. BUT DON'T SKIP IT ON MY ACCOUNT. PLEASE...
...GO FLY A KITE.
DO YOU THINK I COULD COME OVER TO YOUR HOUSE? WE COULD PLAY SQUADRON STRANGE.
SQUADRON— *WHAT*? NO. ***NO***. DIDN'T YOU HEAR ME SAY I WAS BUSY? CAN'T YOU TAKE A HINT?
CHRIST, I HATE THIS SCHOOL. EVERYTHING SMELLS LIKE PISS. FIRST GRADE SMELLS LIKE PISS.
SCHOOL BUS
I THOUGHT YOU *LIKED* SQUADRON STRANGE.
MAYBE WE COULD BORROW THE HEAD KEY AND PLAY WITH THAT. WE HAD FUN LAST TIME. REMEMBER?
YEAH, WELL. THINGS HAVE CHANGED. FIND SOMEONE ELSE TO ENTERTAIN YOU.
CAUGHT YOU. YOUR BIG SISTER WOULDN'T LET US PLAY WITH THE HEAD KEY.
BUT YOU DON'T REMEMBER THAT. BECAUSE *YOU* AREN'T *YOU* ANYMORE.
YOU AREN'T BODE. YOU JUST *LOOK* LIKE HIM. I DON'T KNOW *WHO* YOU ARE, BUT I'M *TELLING*. I'M TELLING TYLER AND KINSEY.
SCHOOL BUS
BODE, NNNOOOOO—

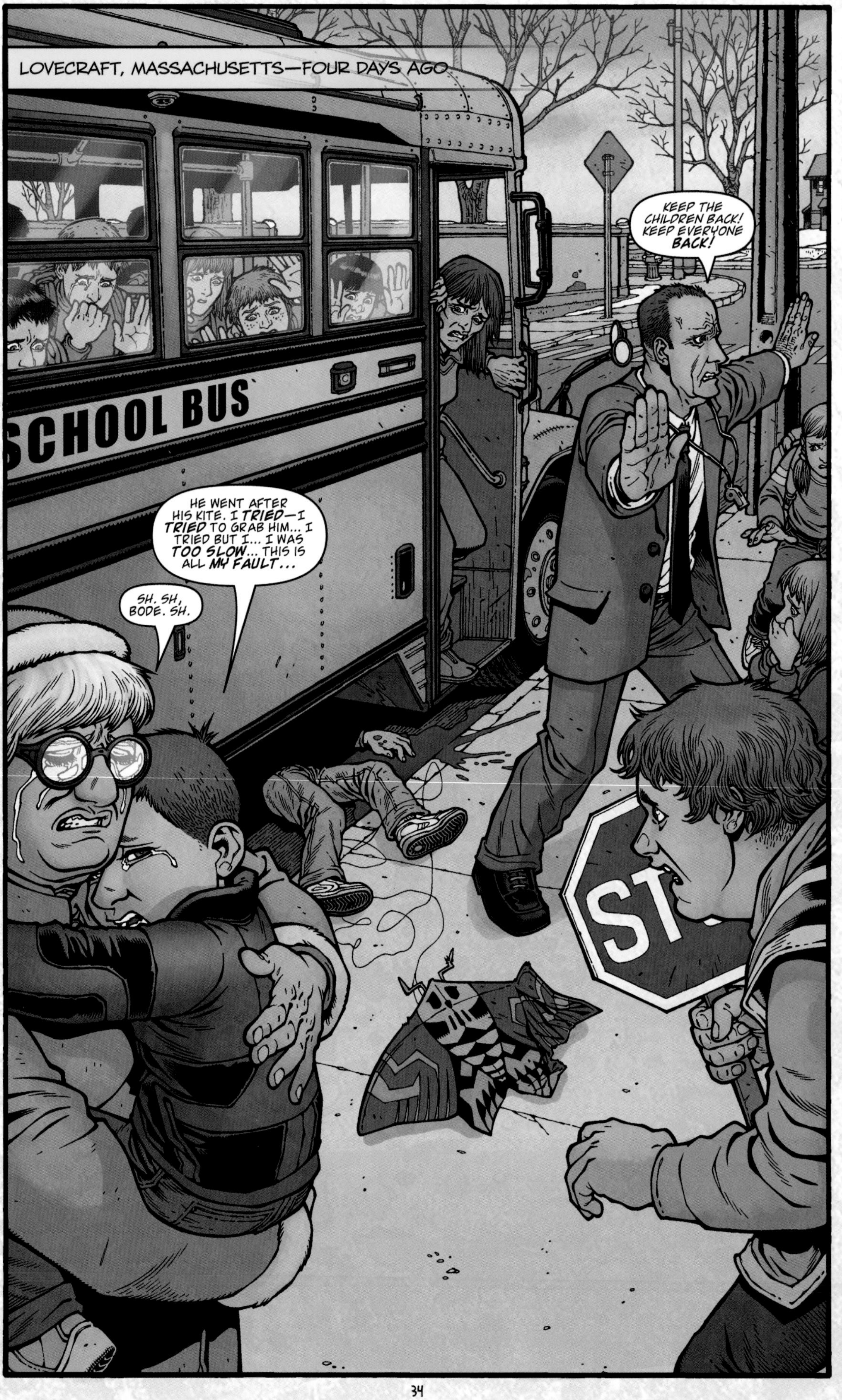
LOVECRAFT, MASSACHUSETTS—FOUR DAYS AGO
KEEP THE CHILDREN BACK! KEEP EVERYONE BACK!
SCHOOL BUS
HE WENT AFTER HIS KITE. I TRIED—I TRIED TO GRAB HIM... I TRIED BUT I... I WAS TOO SLOW... THIS IS ALL MY FAULT...
SH. SH, BODE. SH.
ST

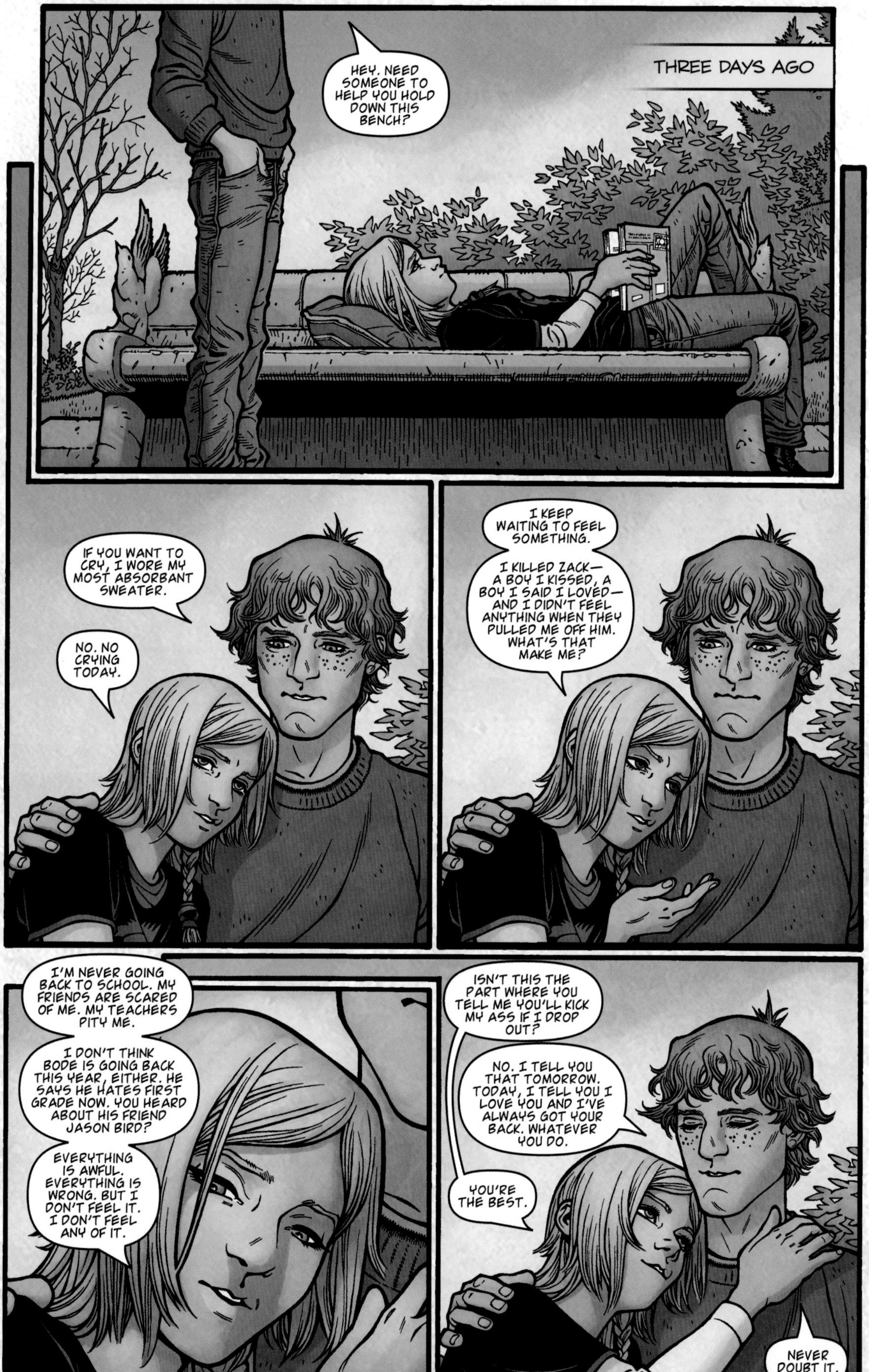
THREE DAYS AGO
HEY. NEED SOMEONE TO HELP YOU HOLD DOWN THIS BENCH?
IF YOU WANT TO CRY, I WORE MY MOST ABSORBANT SWEATER.
NO. NO CRYING TODAY.
I KEEP WAITING TO FEEL SOMETHING.
I KILLED ZACK— A BOY I KISSED, A BOY I SAID I LOVED— AND I DIDN'T FEEL ANYTHING WHEN THEY PULLED ME OFF HIM. WHAT'S THAT MAKE ME?
I'M NEVER GOING BACK TO SCHOOL. MY FRIENDS ARE SCARED OF ME. MY TEACHERS PITY ME.
I DON'T THINK BODE IS GOING BACK THIS YEAR, EITHER. HE SAYS HE HATES FIRST GRADE NOW. YOU HEARD ABOUT HIS FRIEND JASON BIRD?
EVERYTHING IS AWFUL. EVERYTHING IS WRONG. BUT I DON'T FEEL IT. I DON'T FEEL ANY OF IT.
ISN'T THIS THE PART WHERE YOU TELL ME YOU'LL KICK MY ASS IF I DROP OUT?
NO. I TELL YOU THAT TOMORROW. TODAY, I TELL YOU I LOVE YOU AND I'VE ALWAYS GOT YOUR BACK. WHATEVER YOU DO.
YOU'RE THE BEST.
NEVER DOUBT IT.

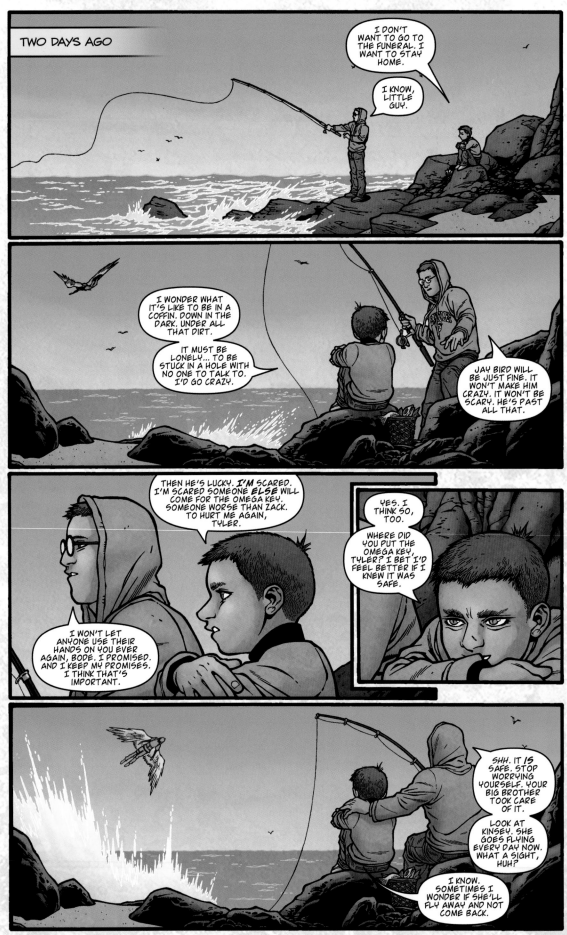

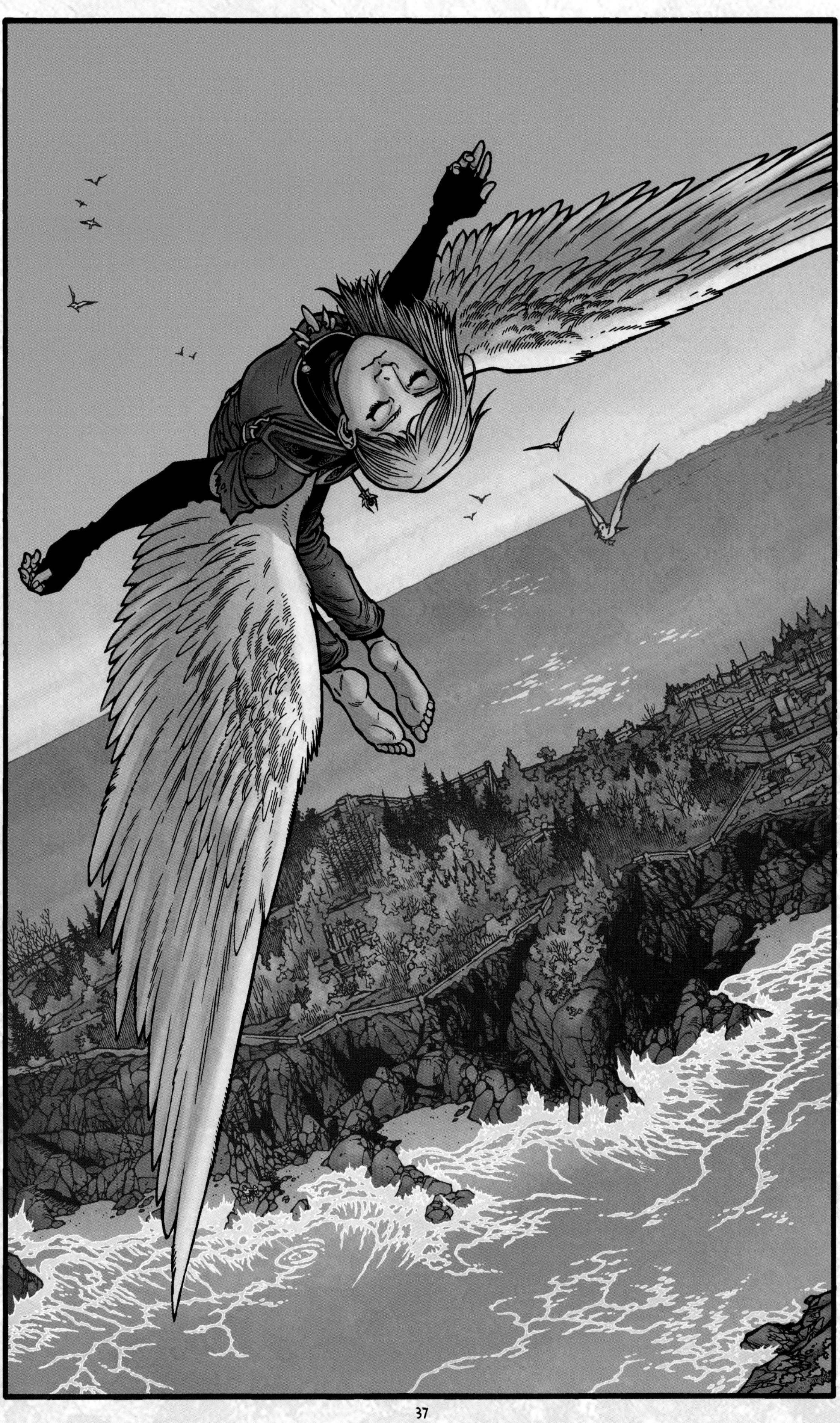

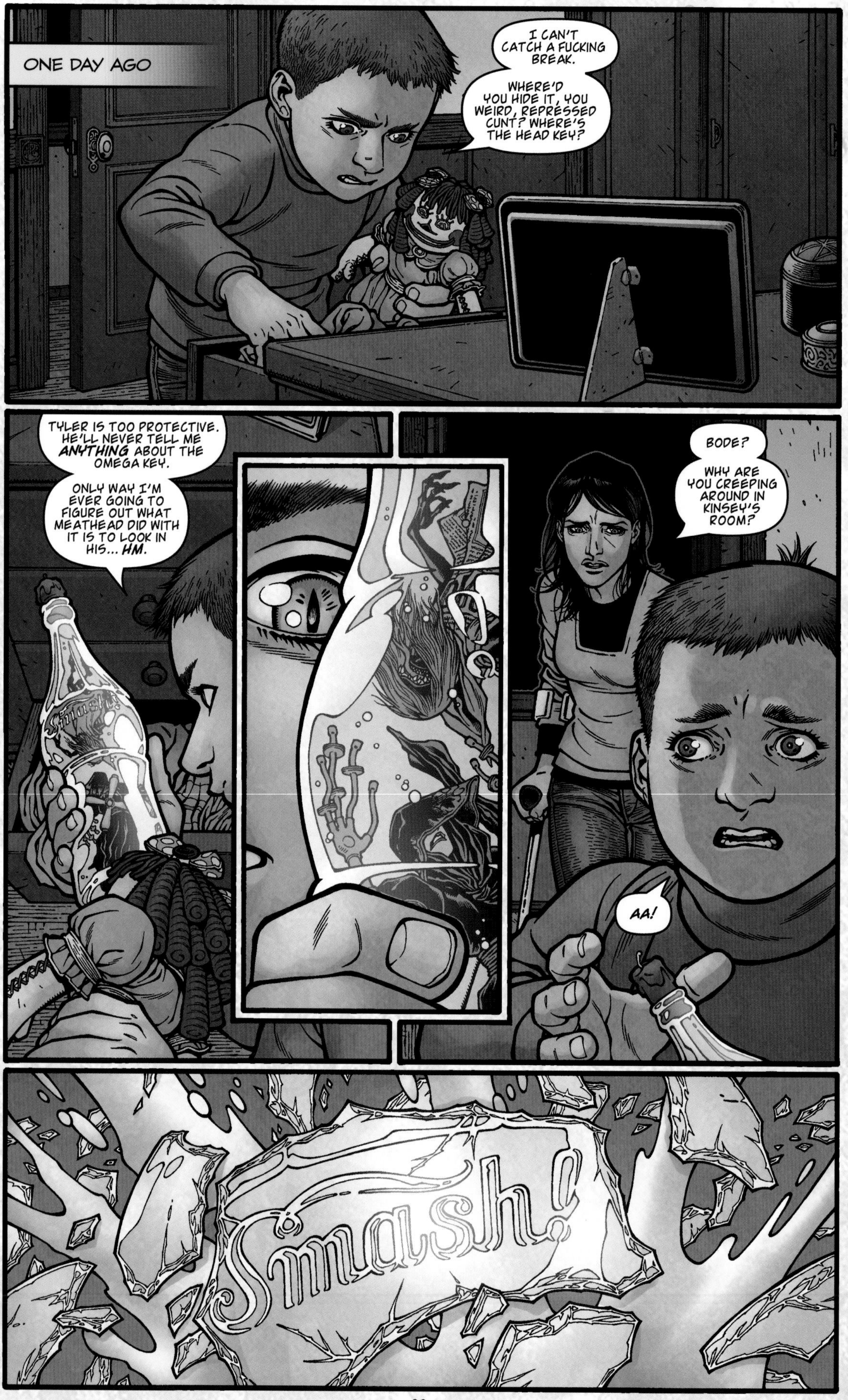
ONE DAY AGO
I CAN'T CATCH A FUCKING BREAK.
WHERE'D YOU HIDE IT, YOU WEIRD, REPRESSED CUNT? WHERE'S THE HEAD KEY?
TYLER IS TOO PROTECTIVE. HE'LL NEVER TELL ME ANYTHING ABOUT THE OMEGA KEY.
ONLY WAY I'M EVER GOING TO FIGURE OUT WHAT MEATHEAD DID WITH IT IS TO LOOK IN HIS... HM.
BODE?
WHY ARE YOU CREEPING AROUND IN KINSEY'S ROOM?
AA!
Smash!

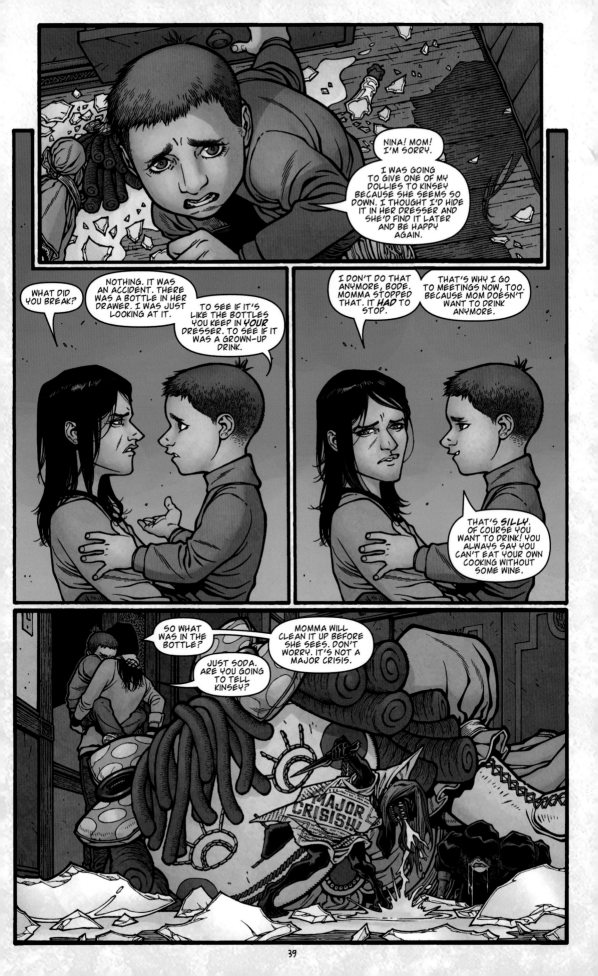

NINA! MOM! I'M SORRY.

I WAS GOING TO GIVE ONE OF MY DOLLIES TO KINSEY BECAUSE SHE SEEMS SO DOWN. I THOUGHT I'D HIDE IT IN HER DRESSER AND SHE'D FIND IT LATER AND BE HAPPY AGAIN.

WHAT DID YOU BREAK?

NOTHING. IT WAS AN ACCIDENT. THERE WAS A BOTTLE IN HER DRAWER. I WAS JUST LOOKING AT IT.

TO SEE IF IT'S LIKE THE BOTTLES YOU KEEP IN *YOUR* DRESSER. TO SEE IF IT WAS A GROWN-UP DRINK.

I DON'T DO THAT ANYMORE, BODE. MOMMA STOPPED THAT. IT *HAD* TO STOP.

THAT'S WHY I GO TO MEETINGS NOW, TOO. BECAUSE MOM DOESN'T WANT TO DRINK ANYMORE.

THAT'S *SILLY*. OF COURSE YOU WANT TO DRINK! YOU ALWAYS SAY YOU CAN'T EAT YOUR OWN COOKING WITHOUT SOME WINE.

SO WHAT WAS IN THE BOTTLE?

MOMMA WILL CLEAN IT UP BEFORE SHE SEES. DON'T WORRY. IT'S NOT A MAJOR CRISIS.

JUST SODA. ARE YOU GOING TO TELL KINSEY?

MAJOR CRISIS!!!

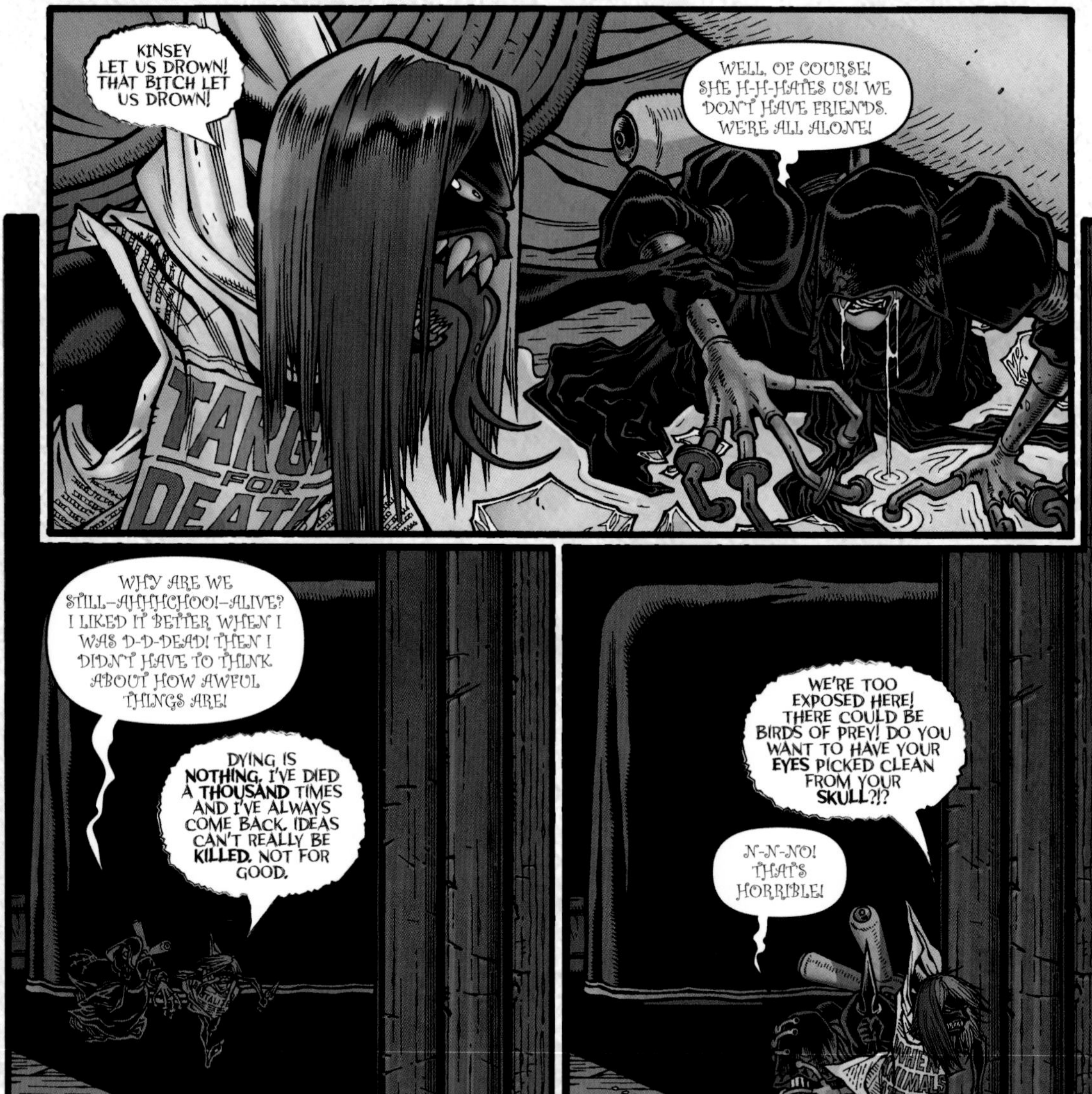
KINSEY LET US DROWN! THAT BITCH LET US DROWN!
WELL, OF COURSE! SHE H-H-HATES US! WE DON'T HAVE FRIENDS. WE'RE ALL ALONE!
WHY ARE WE STILL—AHHHCHOO!—ALIVE? I LIKED IT BETTER WHEN I WAS D-D-DEAD! THEN I DIDN'T HAVE TO THINK ABOUT HOW AWFUL THINGS ARE!
DYING IS **NOTHING**. I'VE DIED A **THOUSAND** TIMES AND I'VE ALWAYS COME BACK. IDEAS CAN'T REALLY BE **KILLED**. NOT FOR GOOD.
WE'RE TOO EXPOSED HERE! THERE COULD BE BIRDS OF PREY! DO YOU WANT TO HAVE YOUR **EYES** PICKED CLEAN FROM YOUR **SKULL**?!?
N-N-NO! THAT'S HORRIBLE!
THEN WE HAVE TO RUN FOR IT!
OH GOD! WE'LL BE FUH-FUH-FLATTENED! THERE'S NO HUH-HUH-HOPE!
SHUT UP! SHUT YOUR FUCKING MOUTH! KEEP RUNNING OR WE'LL BE SMASHED AND THE LAST THING YOU'LL **TASTE** WILL BE YOUR OWN **BRAINS**!
CRUSHED

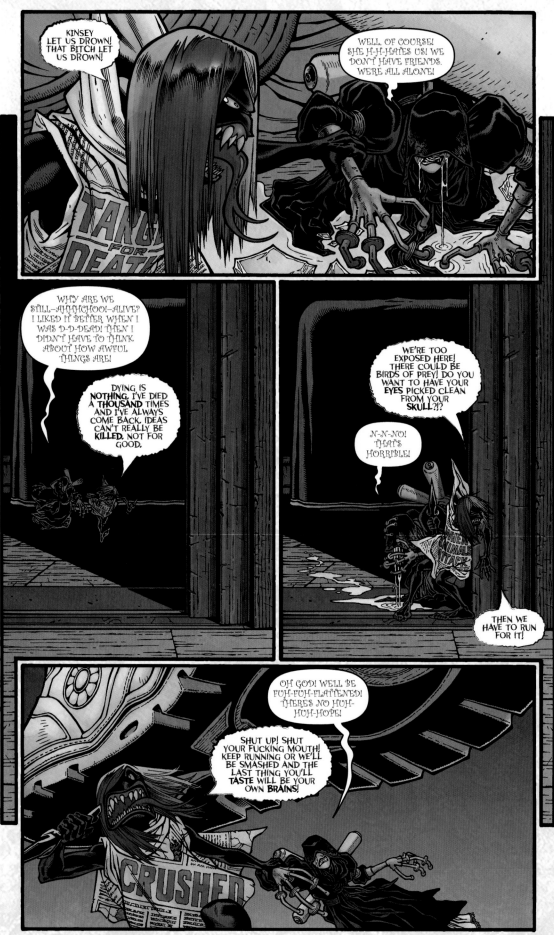

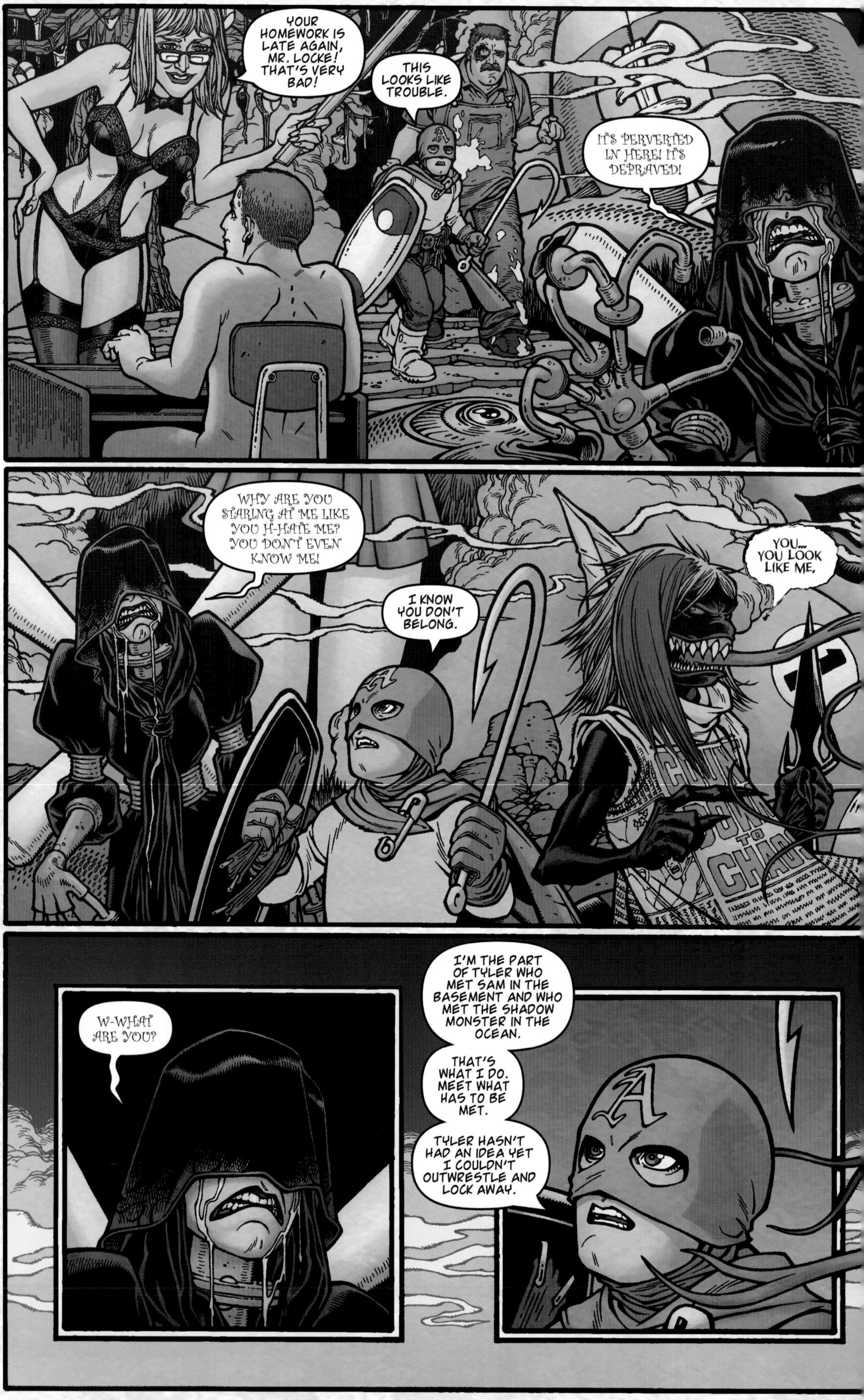
YOUR HOMEWORK IS LATE AGAIN, MR. LOCKE! THAT'S VERY BAD!
THIS LOOKS LIKE TROUBLE.
IT'S PERVERTED IN HERE! IT'S DEPRAVED!
WHY ARE YOU STARING AT ME LIKE YOU H-HATE ME? YOU DON'T EVEN KNOW ME!
I KNOW YOU DON'T BELONG.
YOU... YOU LOOK LIKE ME.
W-WHAT ARE YOU?
I'M THE PART OF TYLER WHO MET SAM IN THE BASEMENT AND WHO MET THE SHADOW MONSTER IN THE OCEAN.
THAT'S WHAT I DO. MEET WHAT HAS TO BE MET.
TYLER HASN'T HAD AN IDEA YET I COULDN'T OUTWRESTLE AND LOCK AWAY.

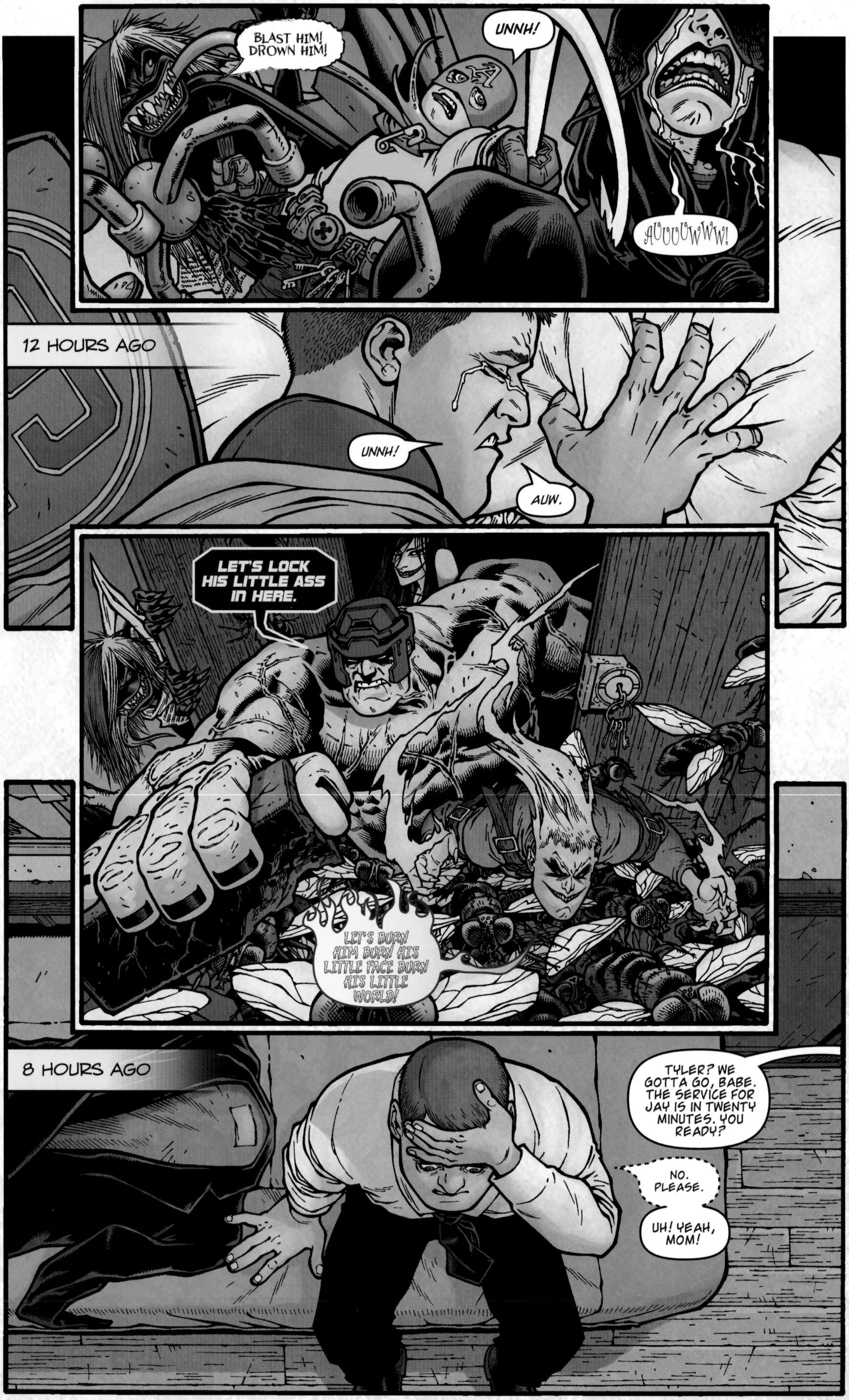
BLAST HIM! DROWN HIM!
UNNH!
AUUUUWWW!
12 HOURS AGO
UNNH!
AUW.
LET'S LOCK HIS LITTLE ASS IN HERE.
LET'S BURN HIM BURN HIS LITTLE FACE BURN HIS LITTLE WORLD!
8 HOURS AGO
TYLER? WE GOTTA GO, BABE. THE SERVICE FOR JAY IS IN TWENTY MINUTES. YOU READY?
NO. PLEASE.
UH! YEAH, MOM!

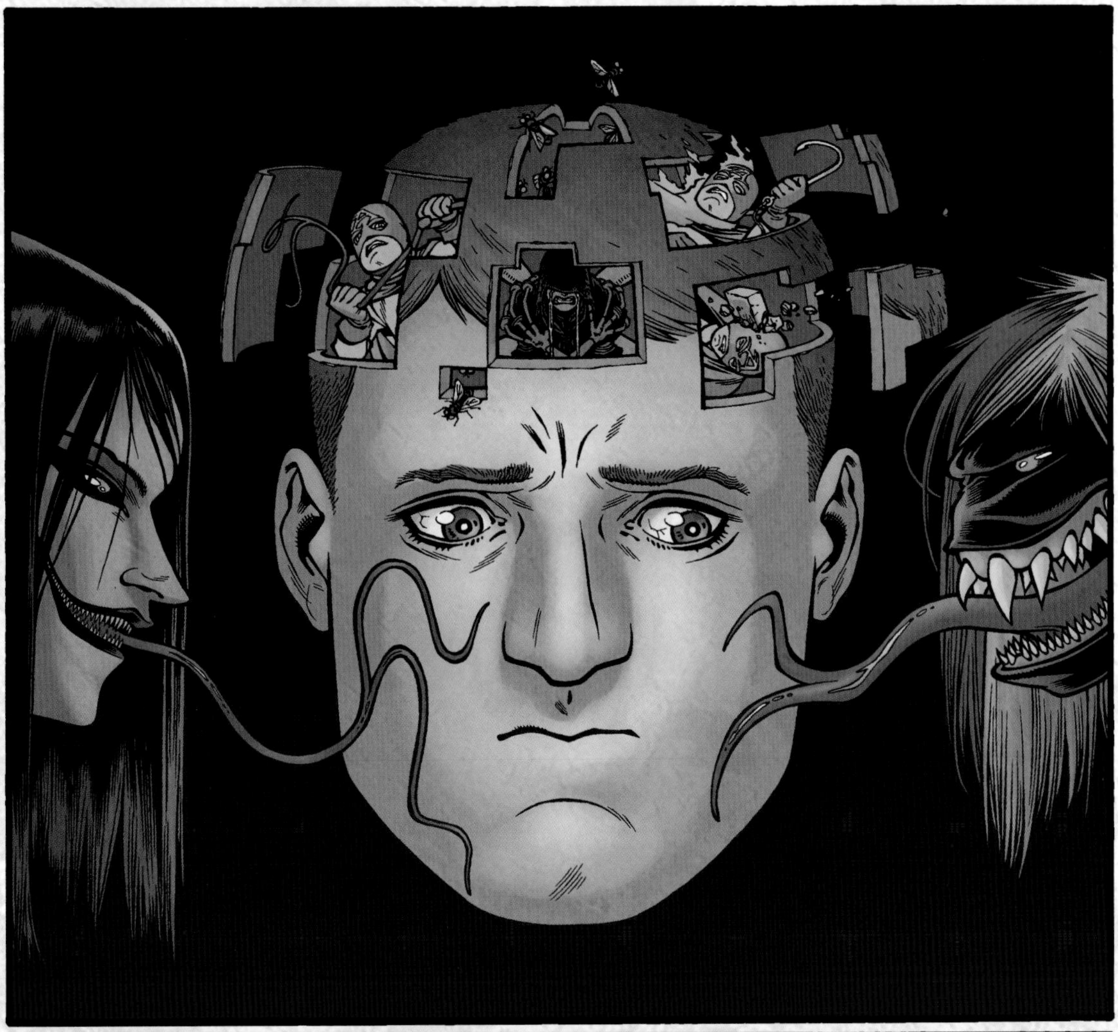

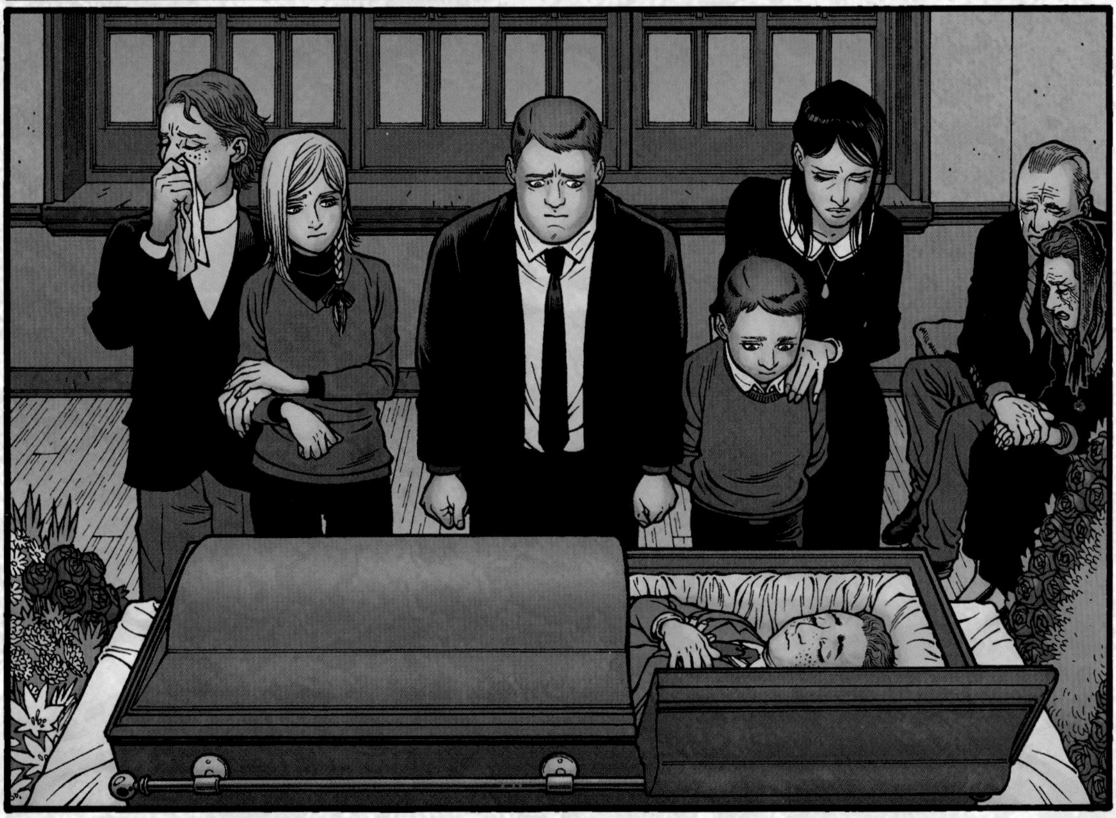

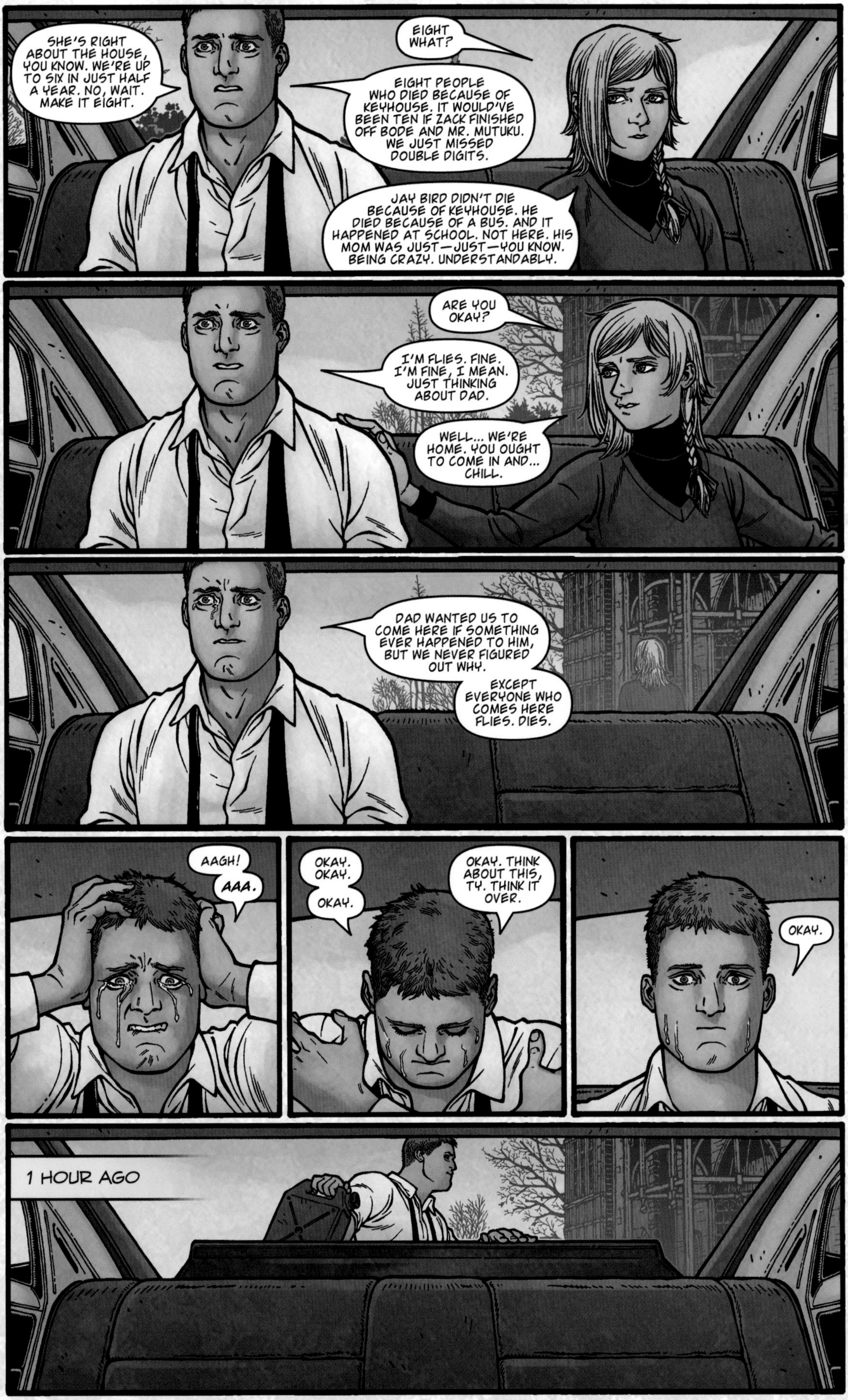
SHE'S RIGHT ABOUT THE HOUSE, YOU KNOW. WE'RE UP TO SIX IN JUST HALF A YEAR. NO, WAIT. MAKE IT EIGHT.
EIGHT WHAT?
EIGHT PEOPLE WHO DIED BECAUSE OF KEYHOUSE. IT WOULD'VE BEEN TEN IF ZACK FINISHED OFF BODE AND MR. MUTUKU. WE JUST MISSED DOUBLE DIGITS.
JAY BIRD DIDN'T DIE BECAUSE OF KEYHOUSE. HE DIED BECAUSE OF A BUS. AND IT HAPPENED AT SCHOOL. NOT HERE. HIS MOM WAS JUST—JUST—YOU KNOW. BEING CRAZY. UNDERSTANDABLY.
ARE YOU OKAY?
I'M FLIES. FINE. I'M FINE, I MEAN. JUST THINKING ABOUT DAD.
WELL... WE'RE HOME. YOU OUGHT TO COME IN AND... CHILL.
DAD WANTED US TO COME HERE IF SOMETHING EVER HAPPENED TO HIM, BUT WE NEVER FIGURED OUT WHY.
EXCEPT EVERYONE WHO COMES HERE FLIES. DIES.
AAGH!
AAA.
OKAY. OKAY.
OKAY.
OKAY. THINK ABOUT THIS, TY. THINK IT OVER.
OKAY.
1 HOUR AGO

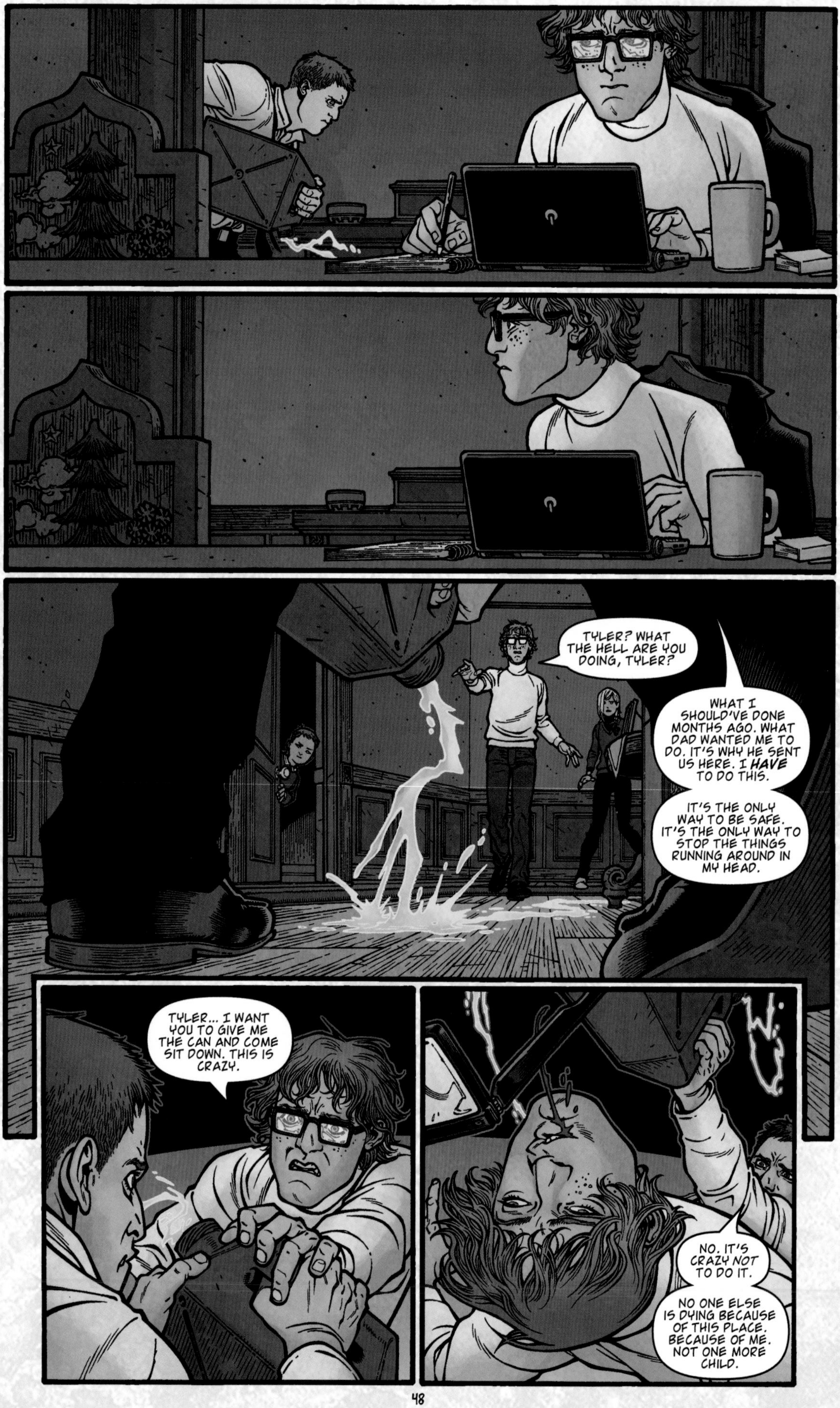
TYLER? WHAT THE HELL ARE YOU DOING, TYLER?
WHAT I SHOULD'VE DONE MONTHS AGO. WHAT DAD WANTED ME TO DO. IT'S WHY HE SENT US HERE. I **HAVE** TO DO THIS.
IT'S THE ONLY WAY TO BE SAFE. IT'S THE ONLY WAY TO STOP THE THINGS RUNNING AROUND IN MY HEAD.
TYLER... I WANT YOU TO GIVE ME THE CAN AND COME SIT DOWN. THIS IS CRAZY.
NO. IT'S *CRAZY NOT* TO DO IT.
NO ONE ELSE IS DYING BECAUSE OF THIS PLACE. BECAUSE OF ME. NOT ONE MORE CHILD.

49

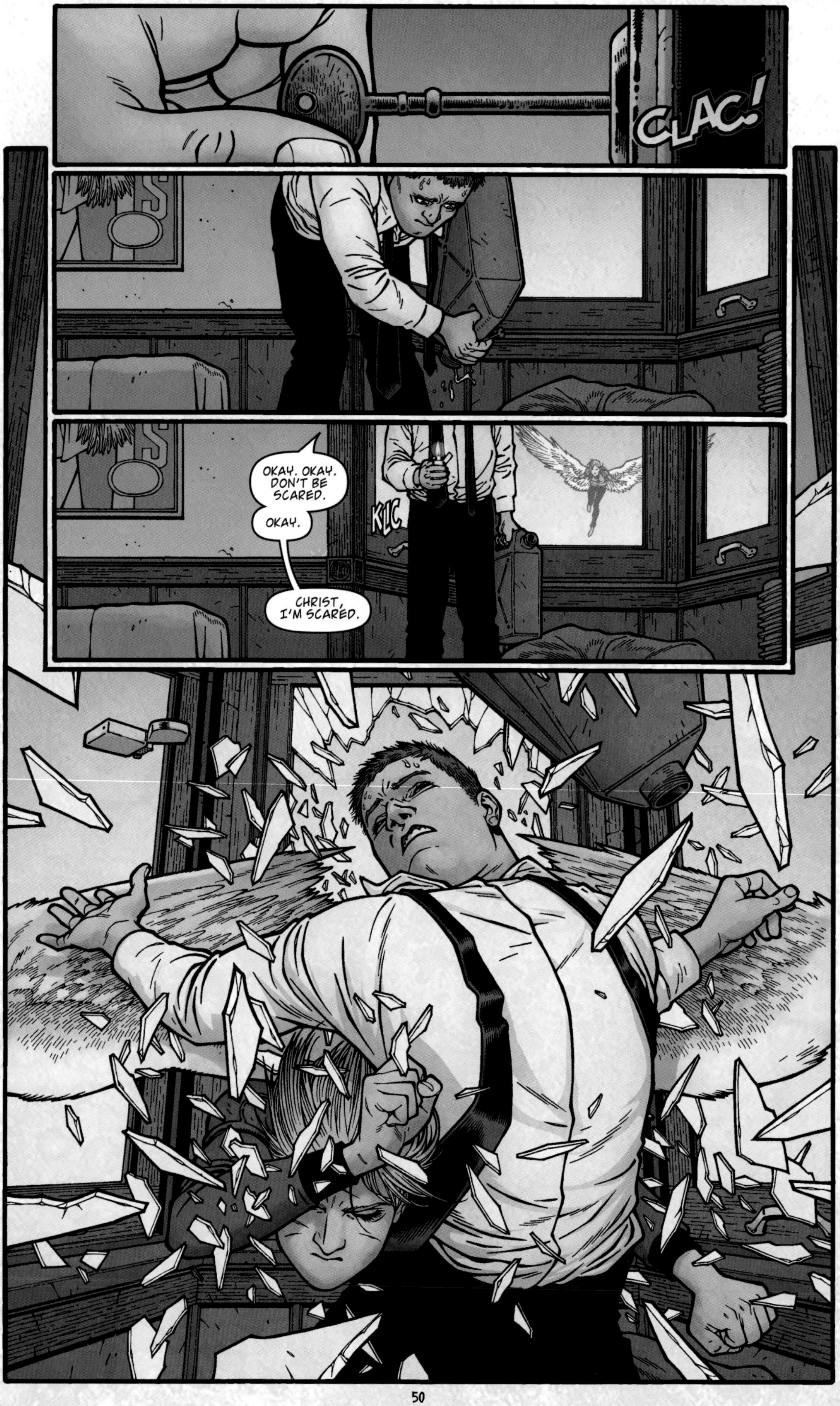
CLAC!
OKAY. OKAY. DON'T BE SCARED.
OKAY.
KLIC
CHRIST, I'M SCARED.

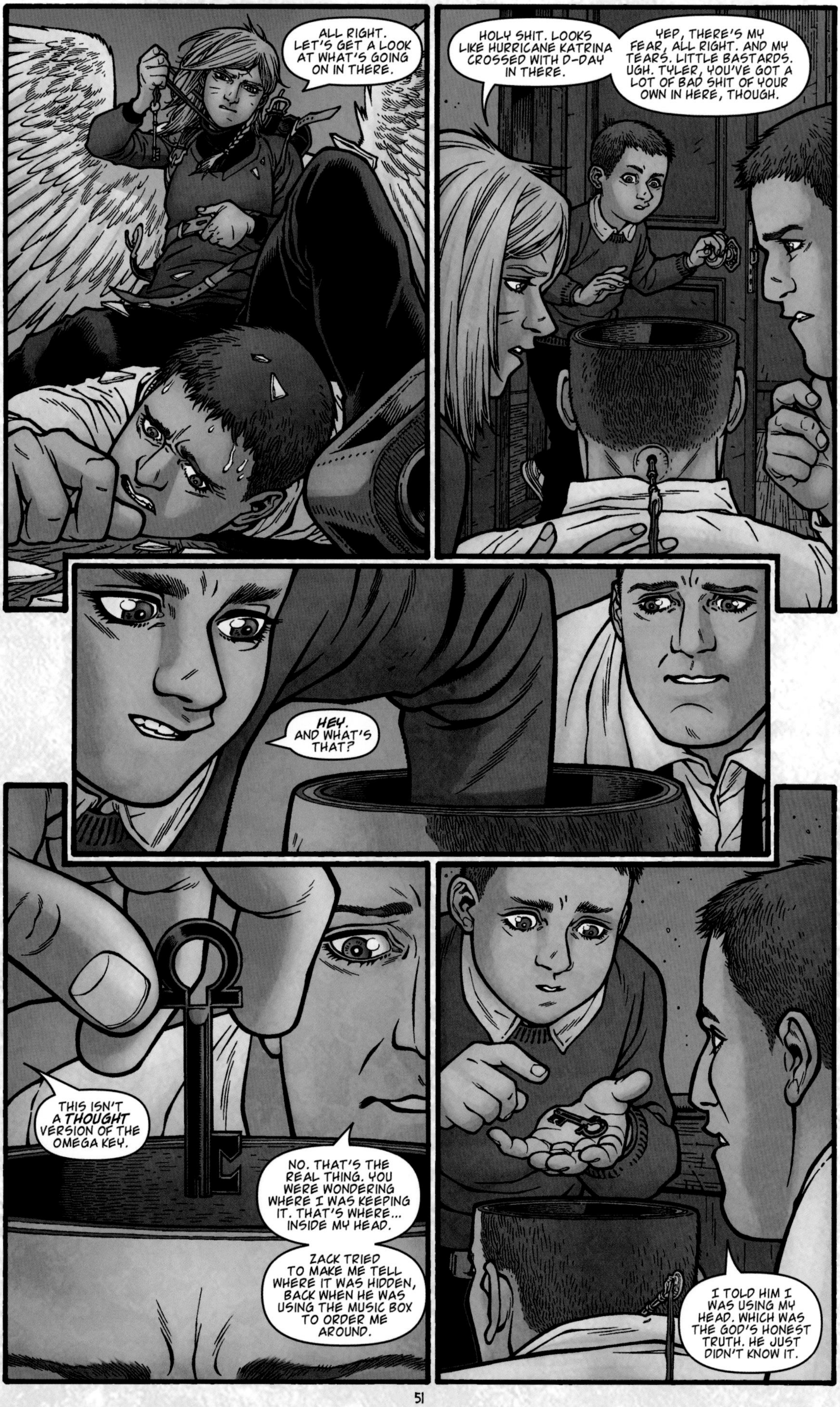
ALL RIGHT. LET'S GET A LOOK AT WHAT'S GOING ON IN THERE.
HOLY SHIT. LOOKS LIKE HURRICANE KATRINA CROSSED WITH D-DAY IN THERE.
YEP, THERE'S MY FEAR, ALL RIGHT. AND MY TEARS. LITTLE BASTARDS. UGH. TYLER, YOU'VE GOT A LOT OF BAD SHIT OF YOUR OWN IN HERE, THOUGH.
HEY. AND WHAT'S THAT?
THIS ISN'T A THOUGHT VERSION OF THE OMEGA KEY.
NO. THAT'S THE REAL THING. YOU WERE WONDERING WHERE I WAS KEEPING IT. THAT'S WHERE... INSIDE MY HEAD.
ZACK TRIED TO MAKE ME TELL WHERE IT WAS HIDDEN, BACK WHEN HE WAS USING THE MUSIC BOX TO ORDER ME AROUND.
I TOLD HIM I WAS USING MY HEAD. WHICH WAS THE GOD'S HONEST TRUTH. HE JUST DIDN'T KNOW IT.

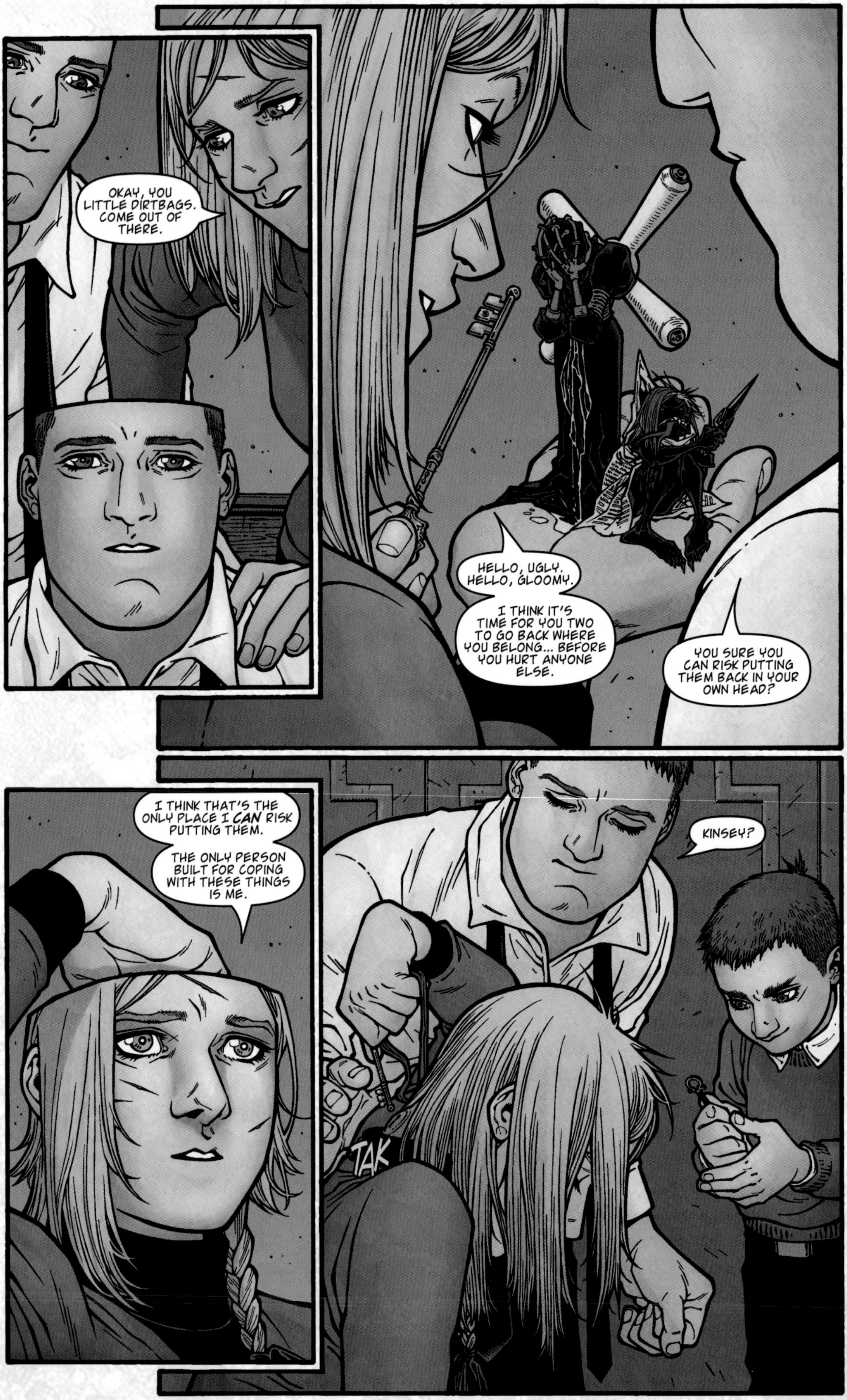
OKAY, YOU LITTLE DIRTBAGS. COME OUT OF THERE.
HELLO, UGLY. HELLO, GLOOMY.
I THINK IT'S TIME FOR YOU TWO TO GO BACK WHERE YOU BELONG... BEFORE YOU HURT ANYONE ELSE.
YOU SURE YOU CAN RISK PUTTING THEM BACK IN YOUR OWN HEAD?
I THINK THAT'S THE ONLY PLACE I *CAN* RISK PUTTING THEM.
THE ONLY PERSON BUILT FOR COPING WITH THESE THINGS IS ME.
KINSEY?
TAK

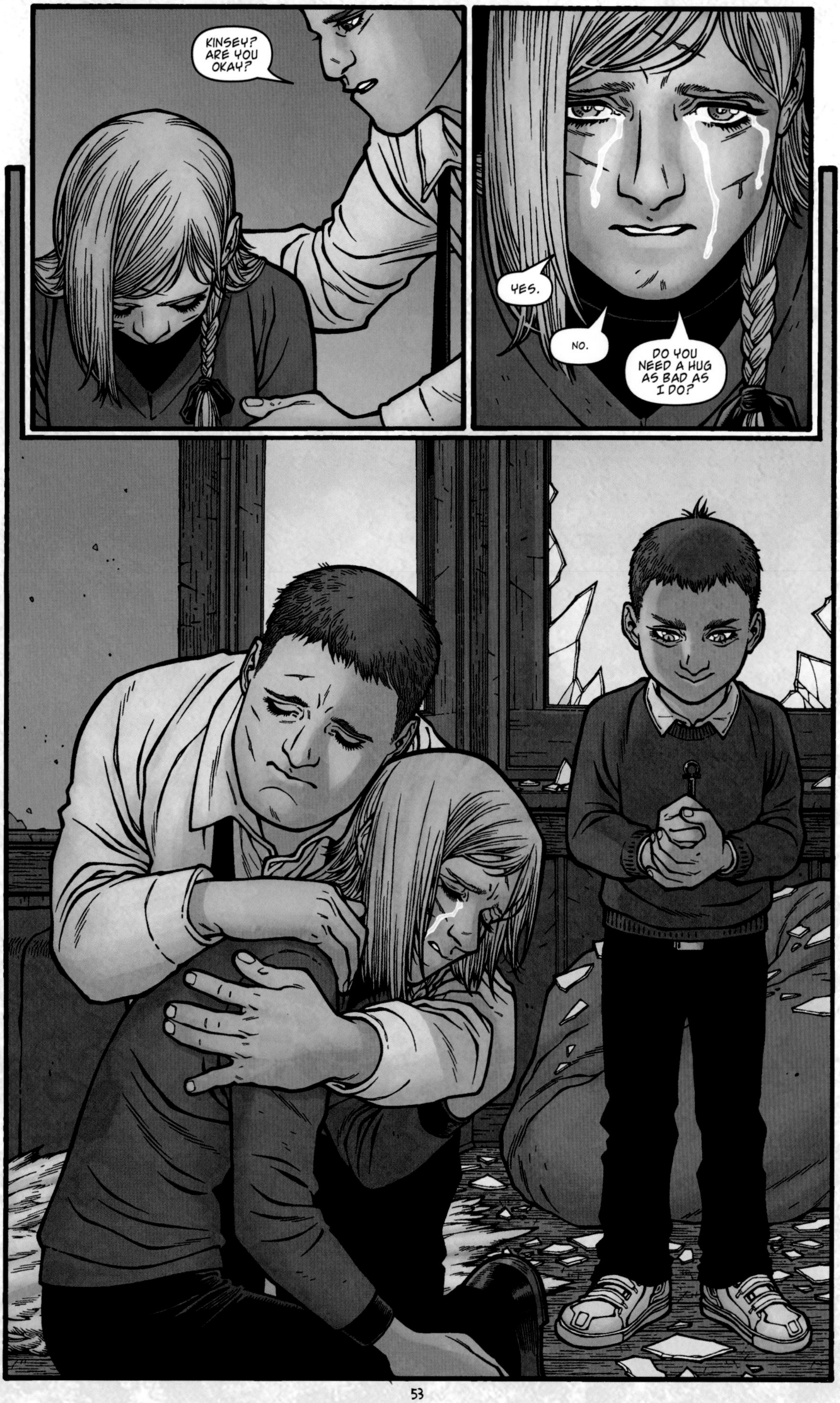
KINSEY? ARE YOU OKAY?
YES.
NO.
DO YOU NEED A HUG AS BAD AS I DO?

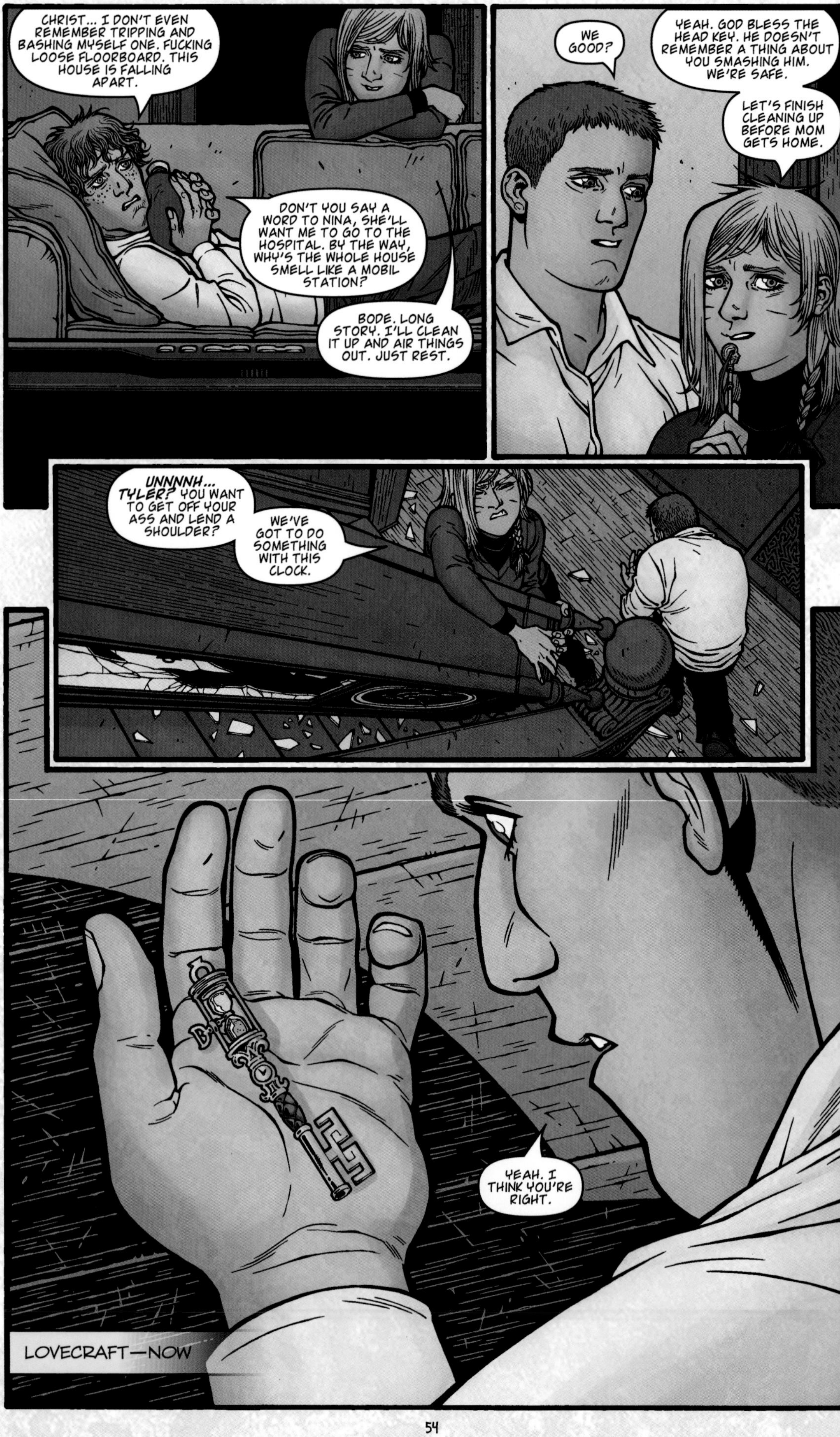

CHRIST... I DON'T EVEN REMEMBER TRIPPING AND BASHING MYSELF ONE. FUCKING LOOSE FLOORBOARD. THIS HOUSE IS FALLING APART.
DON'T YOU SAY A WORD TO NINA, SHE'LL WANT ME TO GO TO THE HOSPITAL. BY THE WAY, WHY'S THE WHOLE HOUSE SMELL LIKE A MOBIL STATION?
BODE. LONG STORY. I'LL CLEAN IT UP AND AIR THINGS OUT. JUST REST.
WE GOOD?
YEAH. GOD BLESS THE HEAD KEY. HE DOESN'T REMEMBER A THING ABOUT YOU SMASHING HIM. WE'RE SAFE.
LET'S FINISH CLEANING UP BEFORE MOM GETS HOME.
UNNNNH... TYLER? YOU WANT TO GET OFF YOUR ASS AND LEND A SHOULDER?
WE'VE GOT TO DO SOMETHING WITH THIS CLOCK.
YEAH. I THINK YOU'RE RIGHT.
LOVECRAFT—NOW

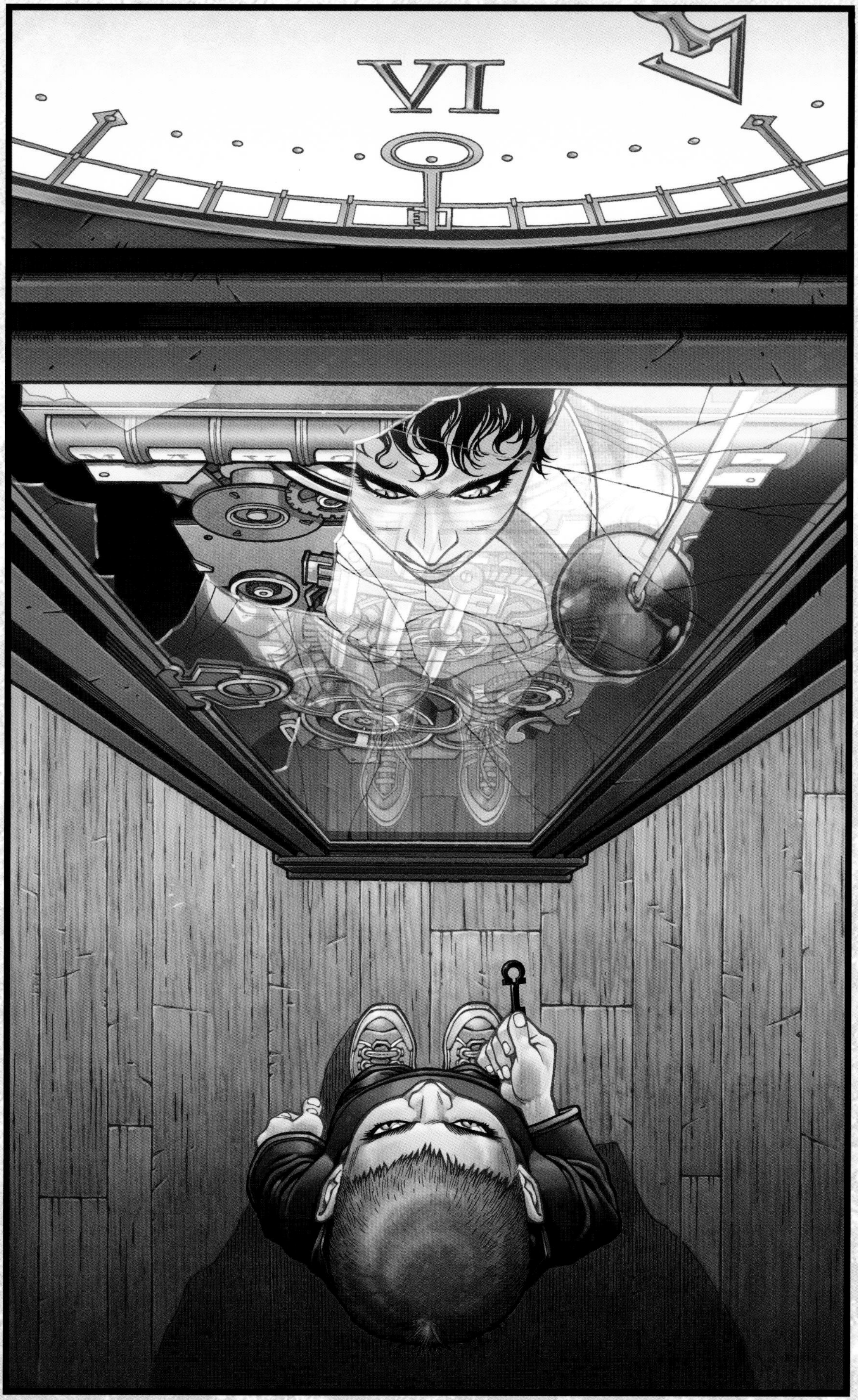

- CLOCKWORKS -

Chapter Three

THE TAMERS OF THE TEMPEST

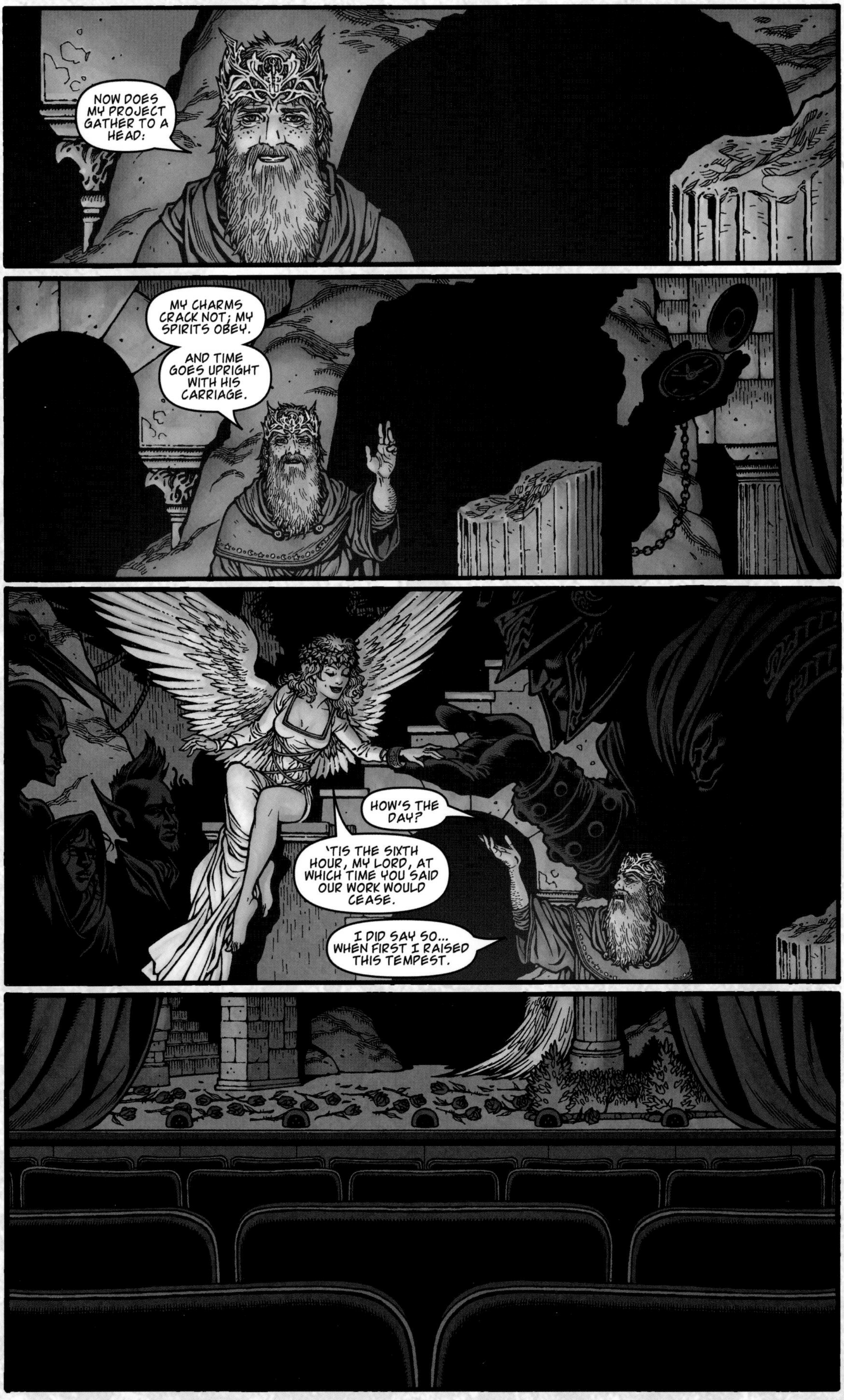
NOW DOES MY PROJECT GATHER TO A HEAD:
MY CHARMS CRACK NOT; MY SPIRITS OBEY.
AND TIME GOES UPRIGHT WITH HIS CARRIAGE.
HOW'S THE DAY?
'TIS THE SIXTH HOUR, MY LORD, AT WHICH TIME YOU SAID OUR WORK WOULD CEASE.
I DID SAY SO... WHEN FIRST I RAISED THIS TEMPEST.

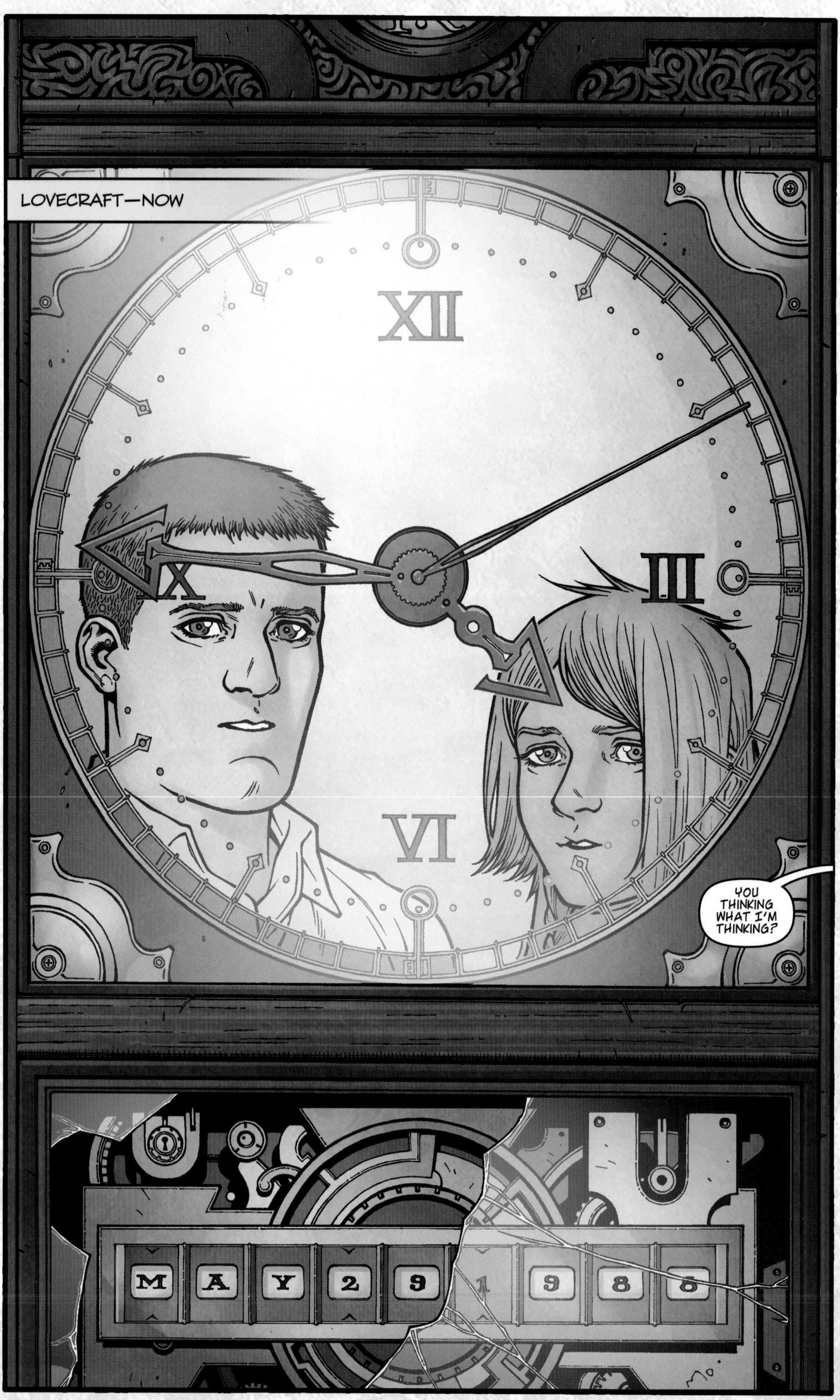
LOVECRAFT—NOW
YOU THINKING WHAT I'M THINKING?
XII
III
VI
X
M A Y 2 9 1 9 8 8

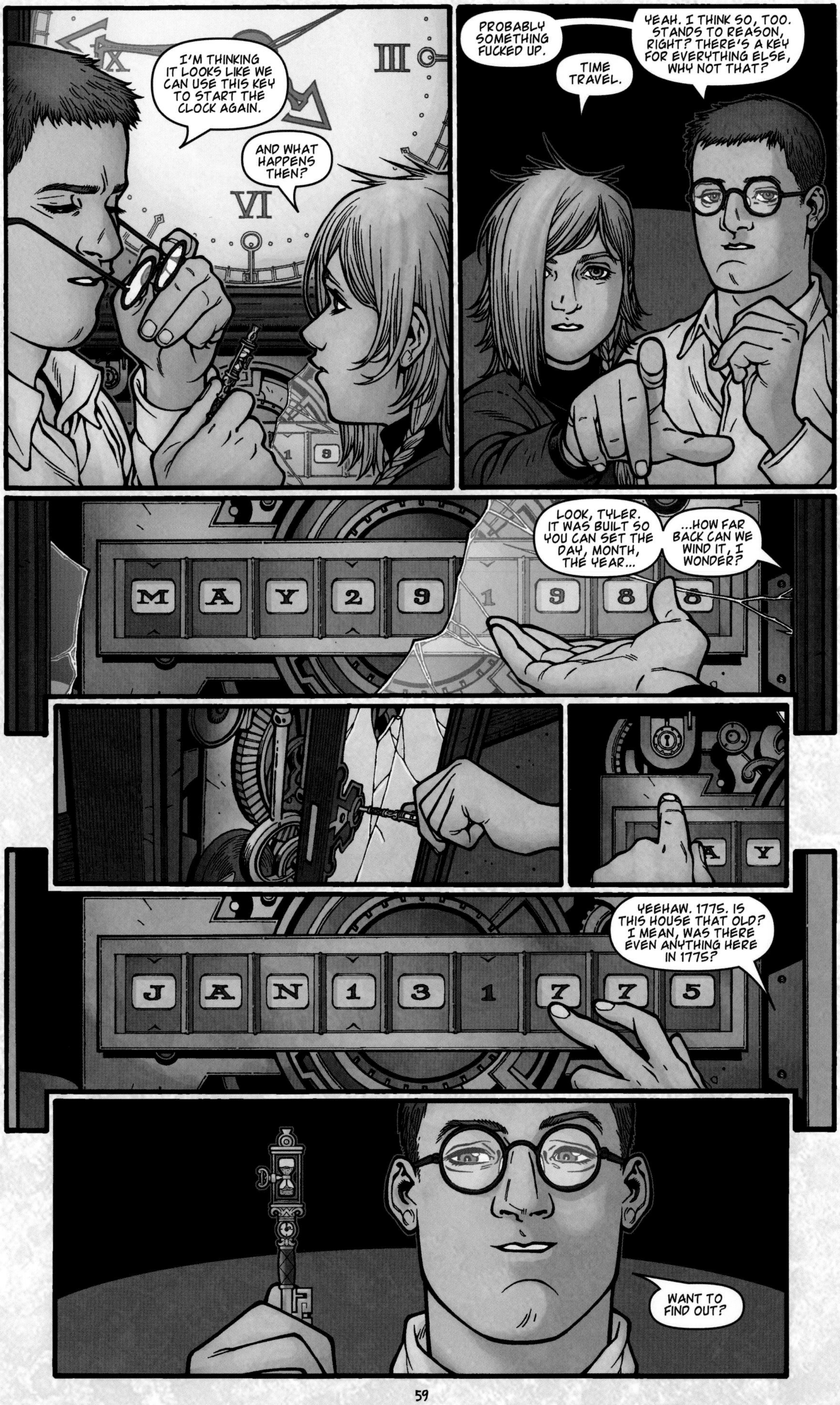
I'M THINKING IT LOOKS LIKE WE CAN USE THIS KEY TO START THE CLOCK AGAIN.
AND WHAT HAPPENS THEN?
PROBABLY SOMETHING FUCKED UP.
TIME TRAVEL.
YEAH. I THINK SO, TOO. STANDS TO REASON, RIGHT? THERE'S A KEY FOR EVERYTHING ELSE, WHY NOT THAT?
M A Y 2 9 1 9 8 8
LOOK, TYLER. IT WAS BUILT SO YOU CAN SET THE DAY, MONTH, THE YEAR...
...HOW FAR BACK CAN WE WIND IT, I WONDER?
J A N 1 3 1 7 7 5
YEEHAW. 1775. IS THIS HOUSE THAT OLD? I MEAN, WAS THERE EVEN ANYTHING HERE IN 1775?
WANT TO FIND OUT?

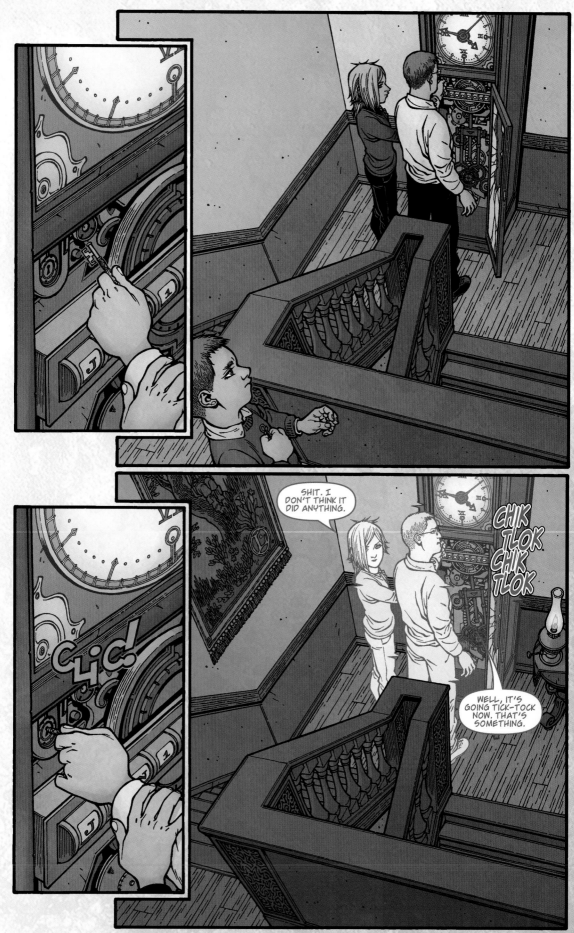

SHIT. I DON'T THINK IT DID ANYTHING.

CHIK TLOK CHIK TLOK

WELL, IT'S GOING TICK-TOCK NOW. THAT'S SOMETHING.

CLICK

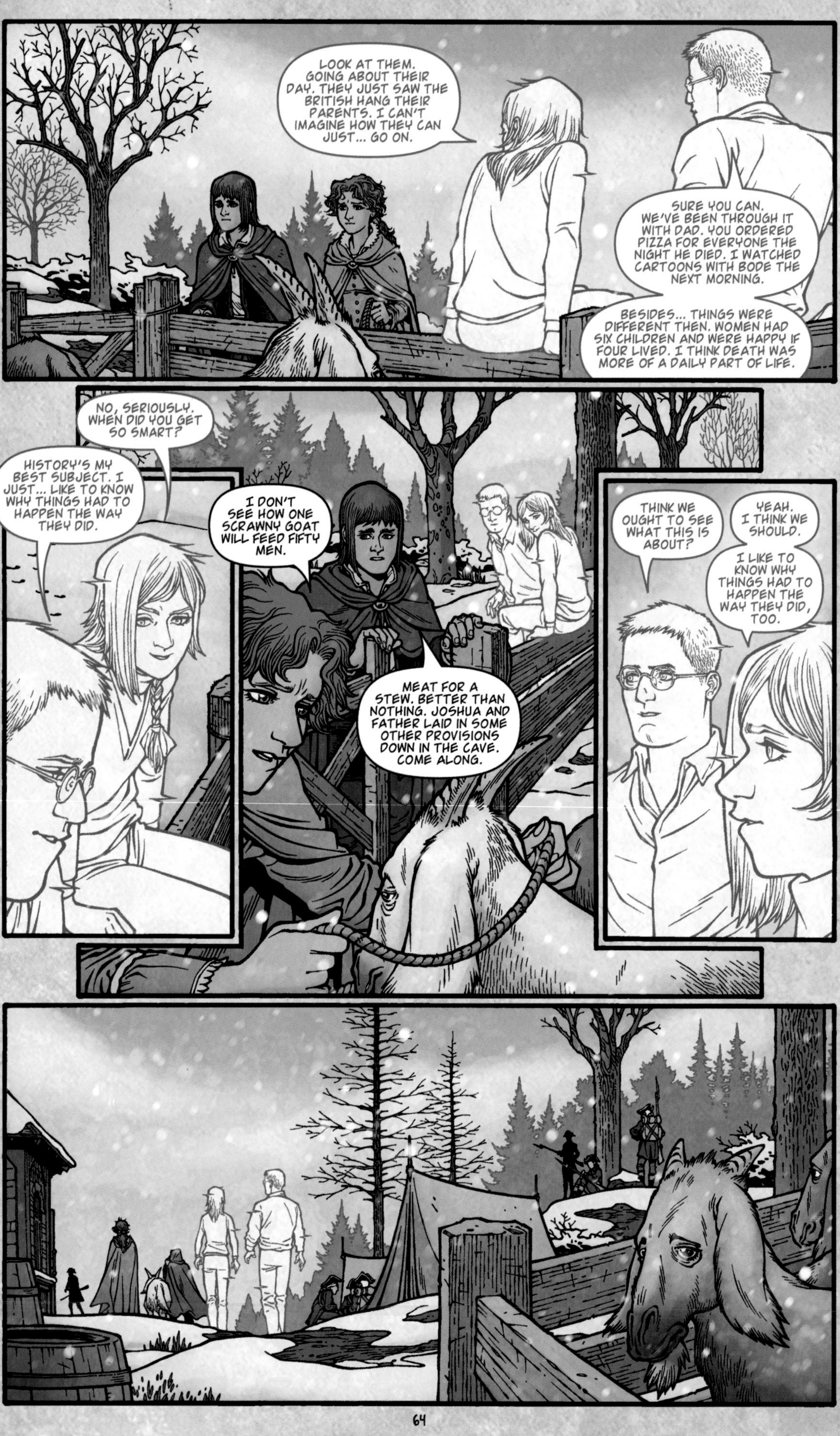
LOOK AT THEM. GOING ABOUT THEIR DAY. THEY JUST SAW THE BRITISH HANG THEIR PARENTS. I CAN'T IMAGINE HOW THEY CAN JUST... GO ON.
SURE YOU CAN. WE'VE BEEN THROUGH IT WITH DAD. YOU ORDERED PIZZA FOR EVERYONE THE NIGHT HE DIED. I WATCHED CARTOONS WITH BODE THE NEXT MORNING.
BESIDES... THINGS WERE DIFFERENT THEN. WOMEN HAD SIX CHILDREN AND WERE HAPPY IF FOUR LIVED. I THINK DEATH WAS MORE OF A DAILY PART OF LIFE.
NO, SERIOUSLY. WHEN DID YOU GET SO SMART?
HISTORY'S MY BEST SUBJECT. I JUST... LIKE TO KNOW WHY THINGS HAD TO HAPPEN THE WAY THEY DID.
I DON'T SEE HOW ONE SCRAWNY GOAT WILL FEED FIFTY MEN.
MEAT FOR A STEW. BETTER THAN NOTHING. JOSHUA AND FATHER LAID IN SOME OTHER PROVISIONS DOWN IN THE CAVE. COME ALONG.
THINK WE OUGHT TO SEE WHAT THIS IS ABOUT?
YEAH. I THINK WE SHOULD.
I LIKE TO KNOW WHY THINGS HAD TO HAPPEN THE WAY THEY DID, TOO.

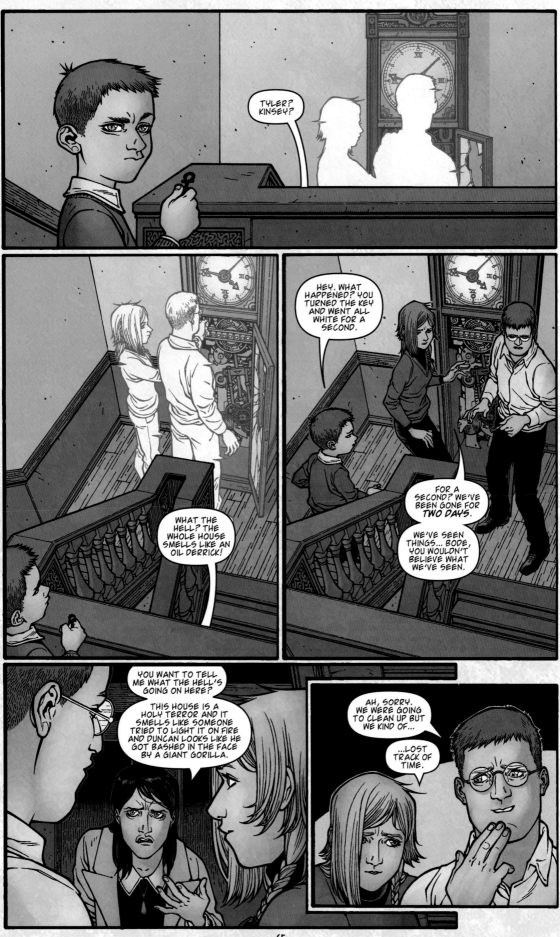

TYLER? KINSEY?

HEY. WHAT HAPPENED? YOU TURNED THE KEY AND WENT ALL WHITE FOR A SECOND.

WHAT THE HELL? THE WHOLE HOUSE SMELLS LIKE AN OIL DERRICK!

FOR A SECOND? WE'VE BEEN GONE FOR TWO DAYS.

WE'VE SEEN THINGS... BODE, YOU WOULDN'T BELIEVE WHAT WE'VE SEEN.

YOU WANT TO TELL ME WHAT THE HELL'S GOING ON HERE?

THIS HOUSE IS A HOLY TERROR AND IT SMELLS LIKE SOMEONE TRIED TO LIGHT IT ON FIRE AND DUNCAN LOOKS LIKE HE GOT BASHED IN THE FACE BY A GIANT GORILLA.

AH, SORRY. WE WERE GOING TO CLEAN UP BUT WE KIND OF...

...LOST TRACK OF TIME.

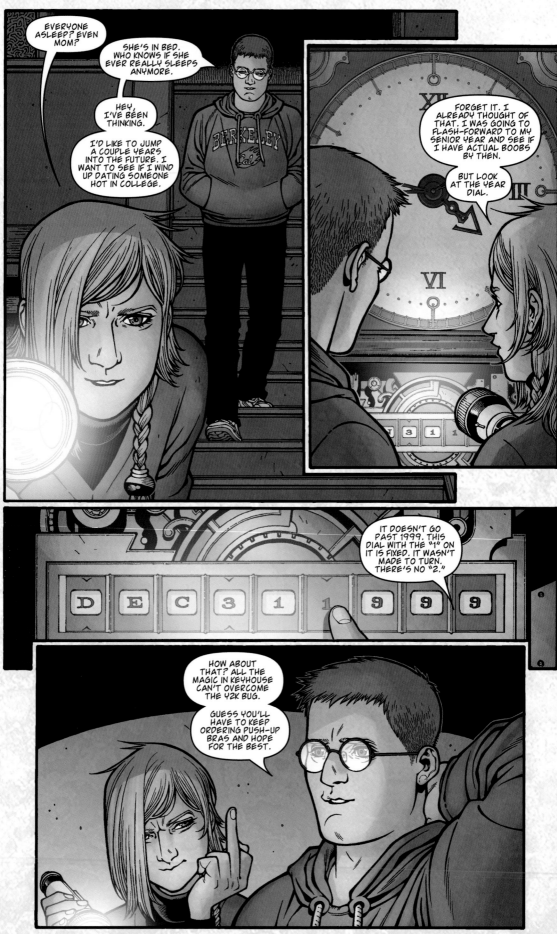

EVERYONE ASLEEP? EVEN MOM?

SHE'S IN BED. WHO KNOWS IF SHE EVER REALLY SLEEPS ANYMORE.

HEY, I'VE BEEN THINKING.

I'D LIKE TO JUMP A COUPLE YEARS INTO THE FUTURE. I WANT TO SEE IF I WIND UP DATING SOMEONE HOT IN COLLEGE.

FORGET IT. I ALREADY THOUGHT OF THAT. I WAS GOING TO FLASH-FORWARD TO MY SENIOR YEAR AND SEE IF I HAVE ACTUAL BOOBS BY THEN.

BUT LOOK AT THE YEAR DIAL.

IT DOESN'T GO PAST 1999. THIS DIAL WITH THE "1" ON IT IS FIXED. IT WASN'T MADE TO TURN. THERE'S NO "2."

DEC 31 1999

HOW ABOUT THAT? ALL THE MAGIC IN KEYHOUSE CAN'T OVERCOME THE Y2K BUG.

GUESS YOU'LL HAVE TO KEEP ORDERING PUSH-UP BRAS AND HOPE FOR THE BEST.

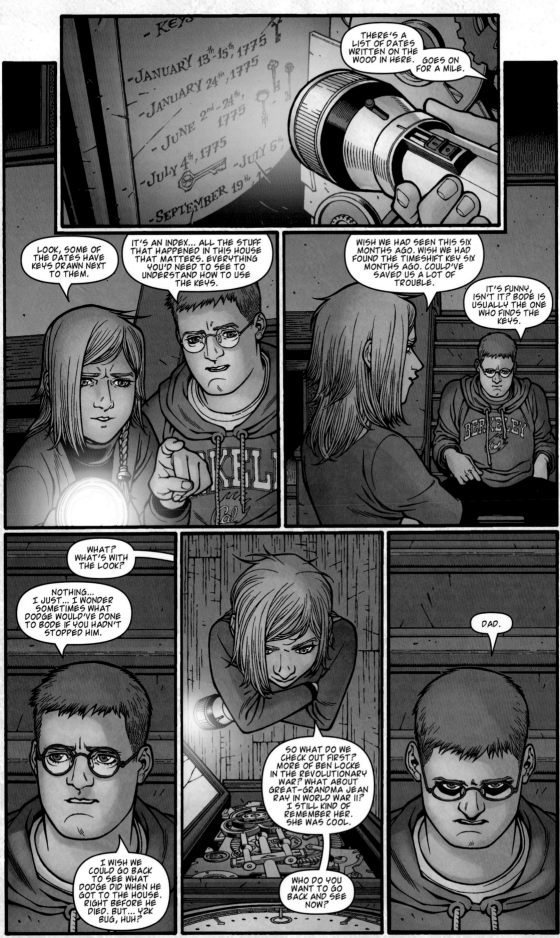

- KEYS -

-JANUARY 13th-15th, 1775
- JANUARY 24th, 1775
- JUNE 2nd -24th, 1775
-JULY 4th, 1775
-JULY 6th,
-SEPTEMBER 19th,

THERE'S A LIST OF DATES WRITTEN ON THE WOOD IN HERE. GOES ON FOR A MILE.

LOOK, SOME OF THE DATES HAVE KEYS DRAWN NEXT TO THEM.

IT'S AN INDEX... ALL THE STUFF THAT HAPPENED IN THIS HOUSE THAT MATTERS. EVERYTHING YOU'D NEED TO SEE TO UNDERSTAND HOW TO USE THE KEYS.

WISH WE HAD SEEN THIS SIX MONTHS AGO. WISH WE HAD FOUND THE TIMESHIFT KEY SIX MONTHS AGO. COULD'VE SAVED US A LOT OF TROUBLE.

IT'S FUNNY, ISN'T IT? BODE IS USUALLY THE ONE WHO FINDS THE KEYS.

WHAT? WHAT'S WITH THE LOOK?

NOTHING... I JUST... I WONDER SOMETIMES WHAT DODGE WOULD'VE DONE TO BODE IF YOU HADN'T STOPPED HIM.

SO WHAT DO WE CHECK OUT FIRST? MORE OF BEN LOCKE IN THE REVOLUTIONARY WAR? WHAT ABOUT GREAT-GRANDMA JEAN RAY IN WORLD WAR II? I STILL KIND OF REMEMBER HER. SHE WAS COOL.

DAD.

I WISH WE COULD GO BACK TO SEE WHAT DODGE DID WHEN HE GOT TO THE HOUSE. RIGHT BEFORE HE DIED. BUT... Y2K BUG, HUH?

WHO DO YOU WANT TO GO BACK AND SEE NOW?

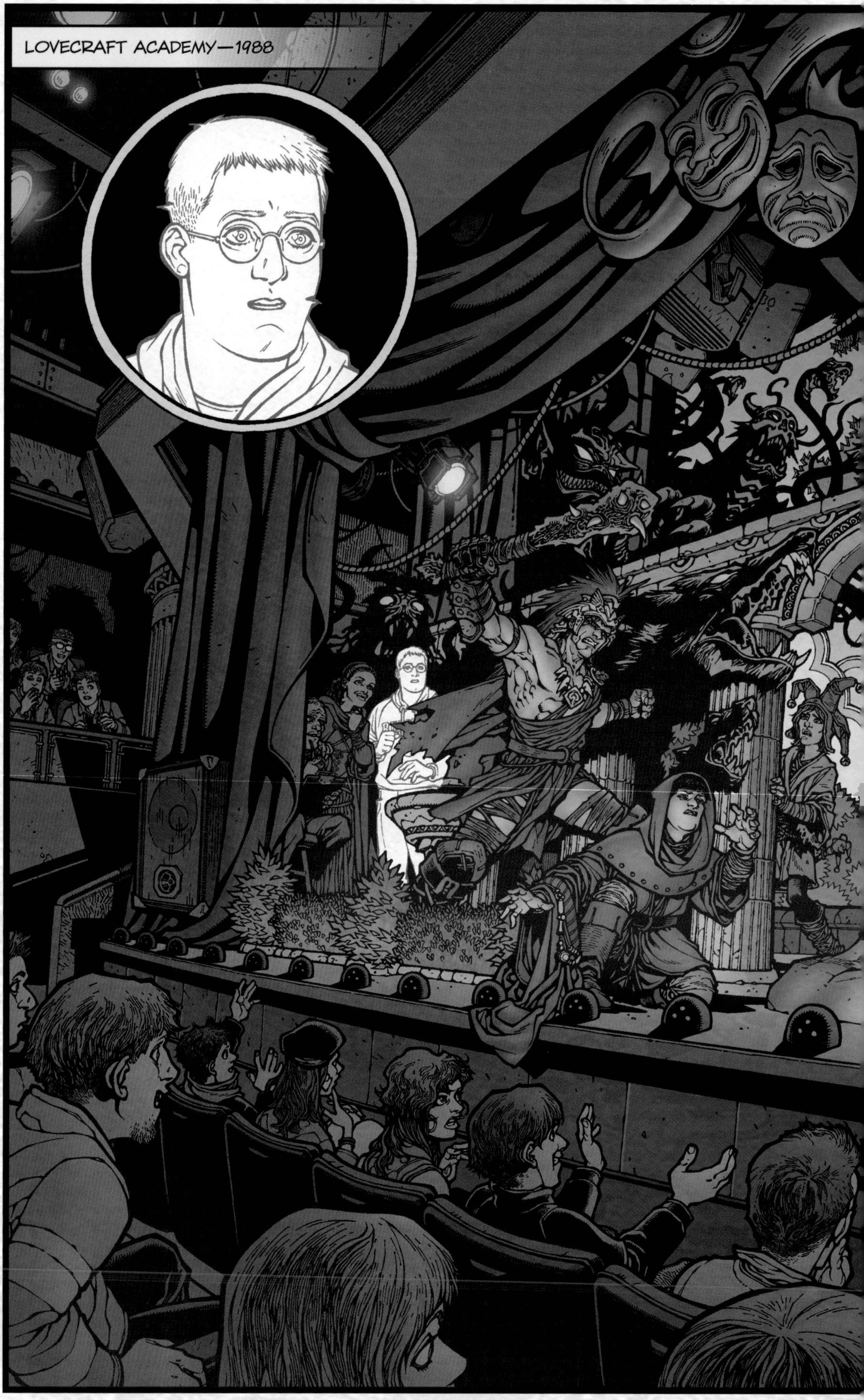
LOVECRAFT ACADEMY—1988

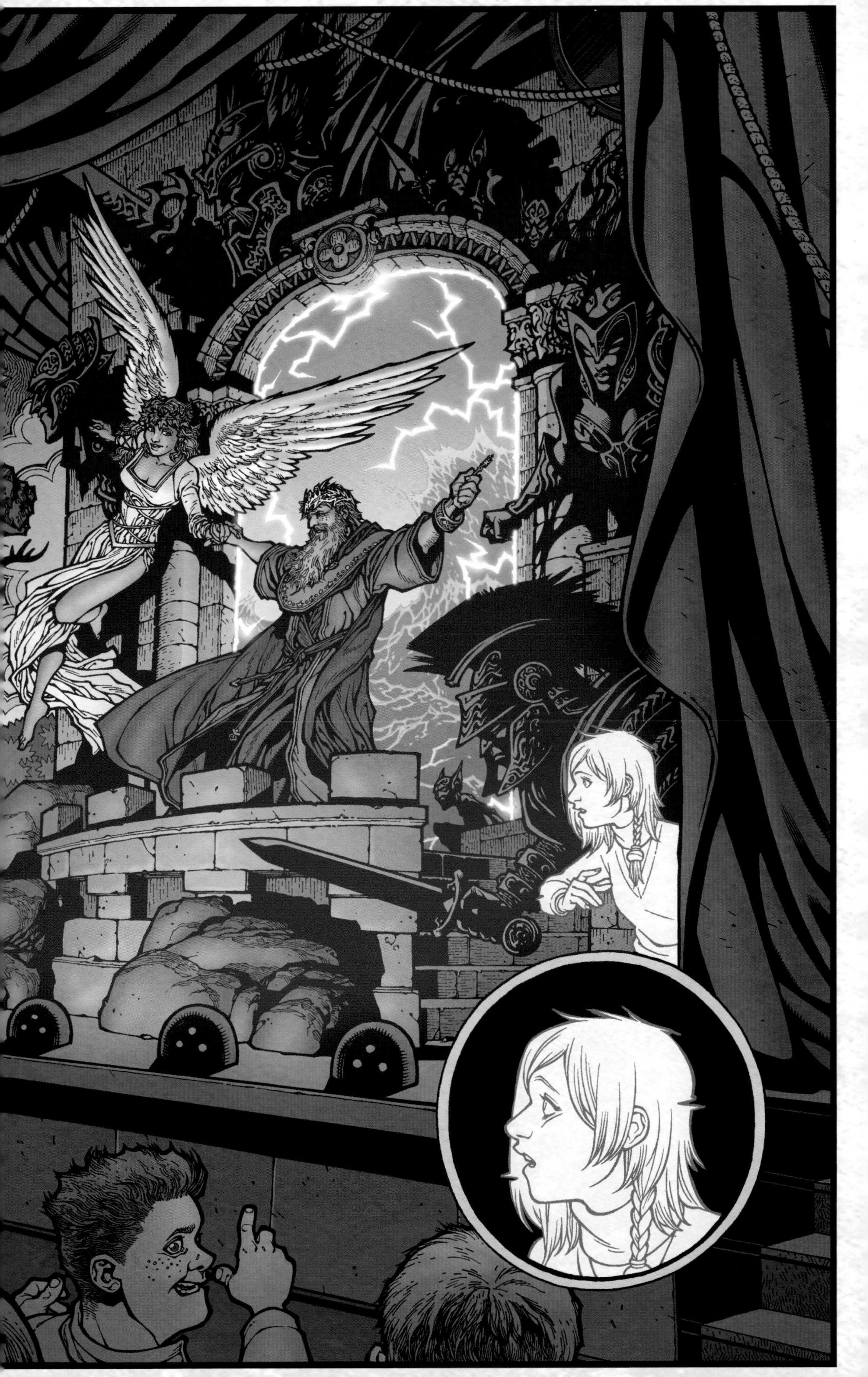

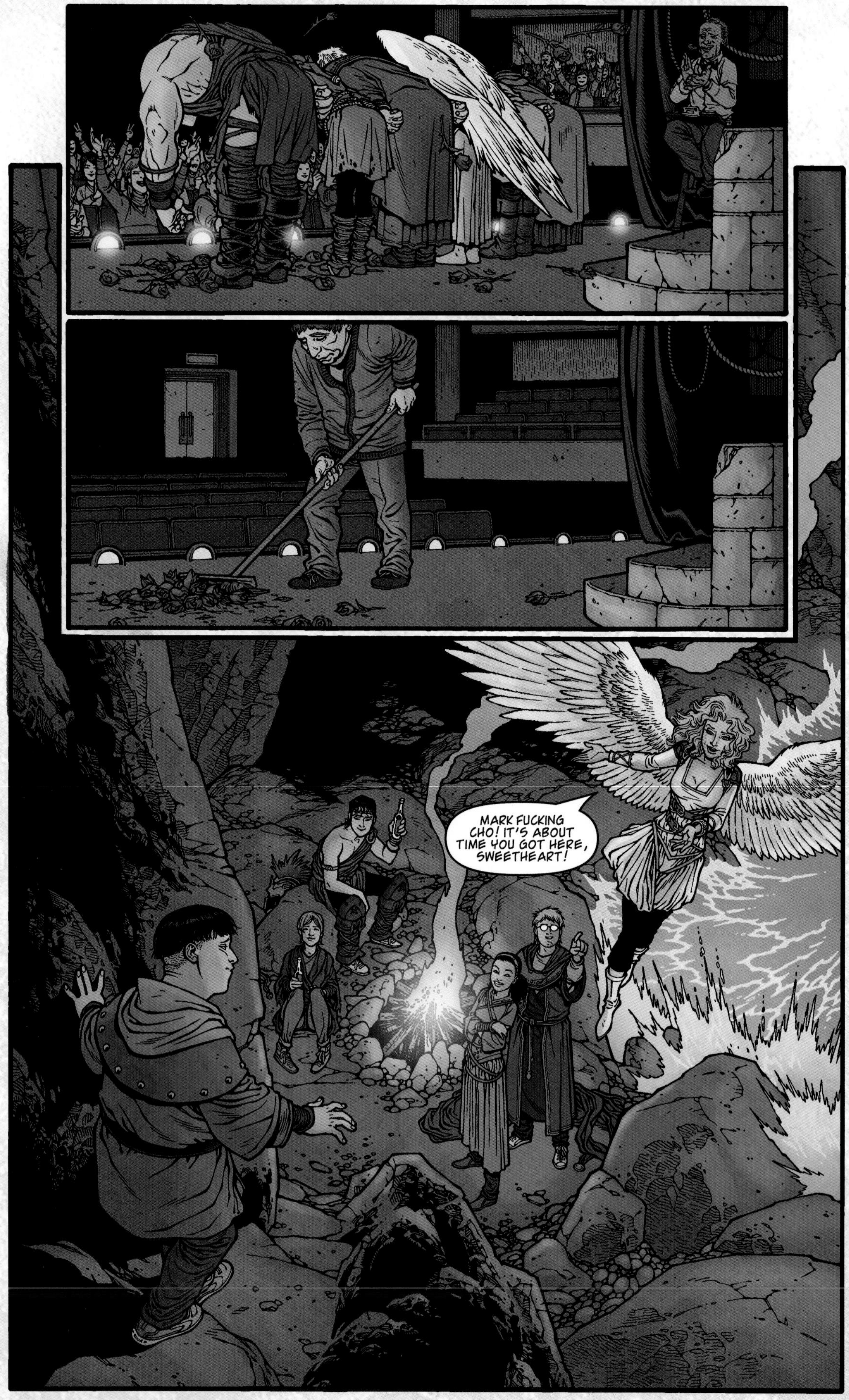
MARK FUCKING CHO! IT'S ABOUT TIME YOU GOT HERE, SWEETHEART!

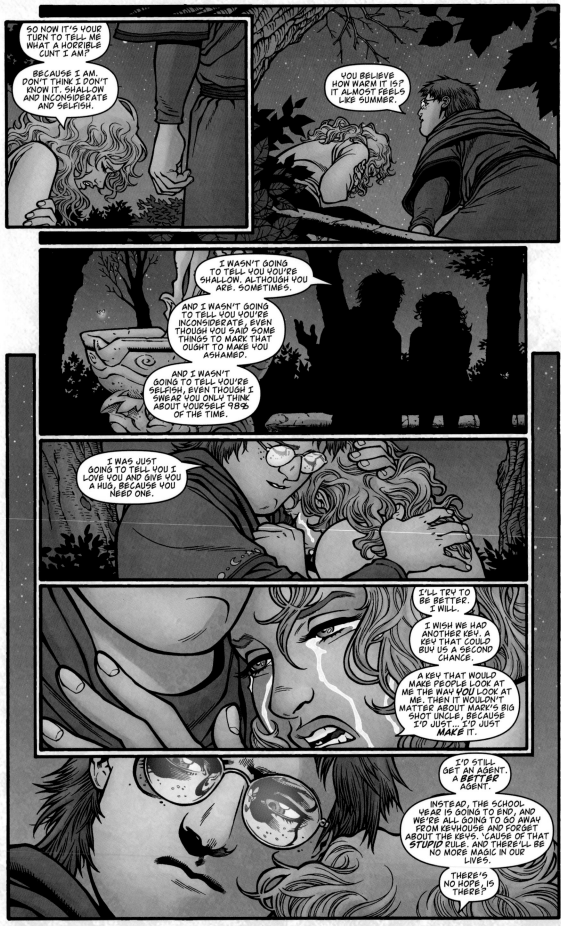

SO NOW IT'S YOUR TURN TO TELL ME WHAT A HORRIBLE CUNT I AM?

BECAUSE I AM. DON'T THINK I DON'T KNOW IT. SHALLOW AND INCONSIDERATE AND SELFISH.

YOU BELIEVE HOW WARM IT IS? IT ALMOST FEELS LIKE SUMMER.

I WASN'T GOING TO TELL YOU YOU'RE SHALLOW. ALTHOUGH YOU ARE. SOMETIMES.

AND I WASN'T GOING TO TELL YOU YOU'RE INCONSIDERATE, EVEN THOUGH YOU SAID SOME THINGS TO MARK THAT OUGHT TO MAKE YOU ASHAMED.

AND I WASN'T GOING TO TELL YOU YOU'RE SELFISH, EVEN THOUGH I SWEAR YOU ONLY THINK ABOUT YOURSELF 98% OF THE TIME.

I WAS JUST GOING TO TELL YOU I LOVE YOU AND GIVE YOU A HUG, BECAUSE YOU NEED ONE.

I'LL TRY TO BE BETTER. I WILL.

I WISH WE HAD ANOTHER KEY. A KEY THAT COULD BUY US A SECOND CHANCE.

A KEY THAT WOULD MAKE PEOPLE LOOK AT ME THE WAY YOU LOOK AT ME. THEN IT WOULDN'T MATTER ABOUT MARK'S BIG SHOT UNCLE, BECAUSE I'D JUST... I'D JUST MAKE IT.

I'D STILL GET AN AGENT. A BETTER AGENT.

INSTEAD, THE SCHOOL YEAR IS GOING TO END, AND WE'RE ALL GOING TO GO AWAY FROM KEYHOUSE AND FORGET ABOUT THE KEYS. 'CAUSE OF THAT STUPID RULE. AND THERE'LL BE NO MORE MAGIC IN OUR LIVES.

THERE'S NO HOPE, IS THERE?

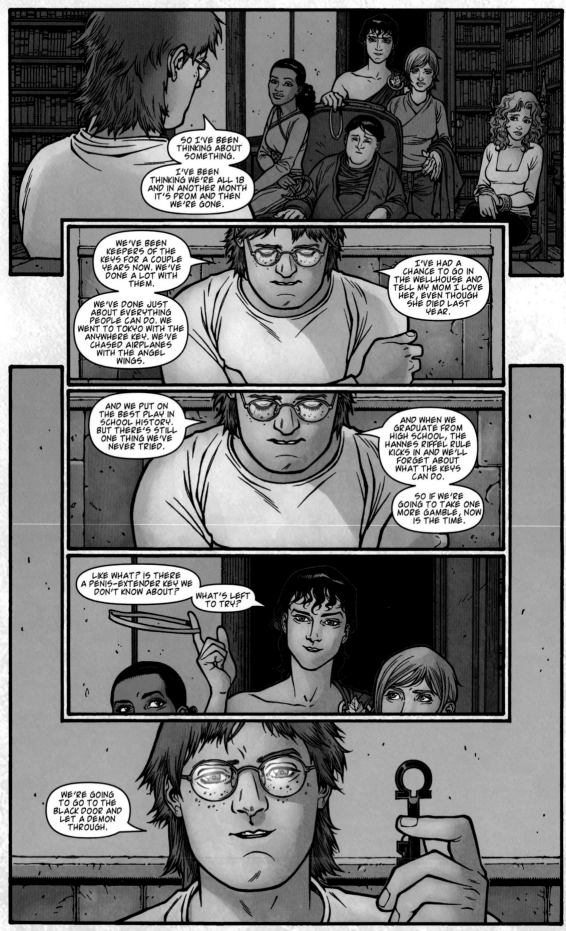

SO I'VE BEEN THINKING ABOUT SOMETHING.

I'VE BEEN THINKING WE'RE ALL 18 AND IN ANOTHER MONTH IT'S PROM AND THEN WE'RE GONE.

WE'VE BEEN KEEPERS OF THE KEYS FOR A COUPLE YEARS NOW. WE'VE DONE A LOT WITH THEM.

WE'VE DONE JUST ABOUT EVERYTHING PEOPLE CAN DO. WE WENT TO TOKYO WITH THE ANYWHERE KEY. WE'VE CHASED AIRPLANES WITH THE ANGEL WINGS.

I'VE HAD A CHANCE TO GO IN THE WELLHOUSE AND TELL MY MOM I LOVE HER, EVEN THOUGH SHE DIED LAST YEAR.

AND WE PUT ON THE BEST PLAY IN SCHOOL HISTORY. BUT THERE'S STILL ONE THING WE'VE NEVER TRIED.

AND WHEN WE GRADUATE FROM HIGH SCHOOL, THE HANNES RIFFEL RULE KICKS IN AND WE'LL FORGET ABOUT WHAT THE KEYS CAN DO.

SO IF WE'RE GOING TO TAKE ONE MORE GAMBLE, NOW IS THE TIME.

LIKE WHAT? IS THERE A PENIS-EXTENDER KEY WE DON'T KNOW ABOUT?

WHAT'S LEFT TO TRY?

WE'RE GOING TO GO TO THE BLACK DOOR AND LET A DEMON THROUGH.

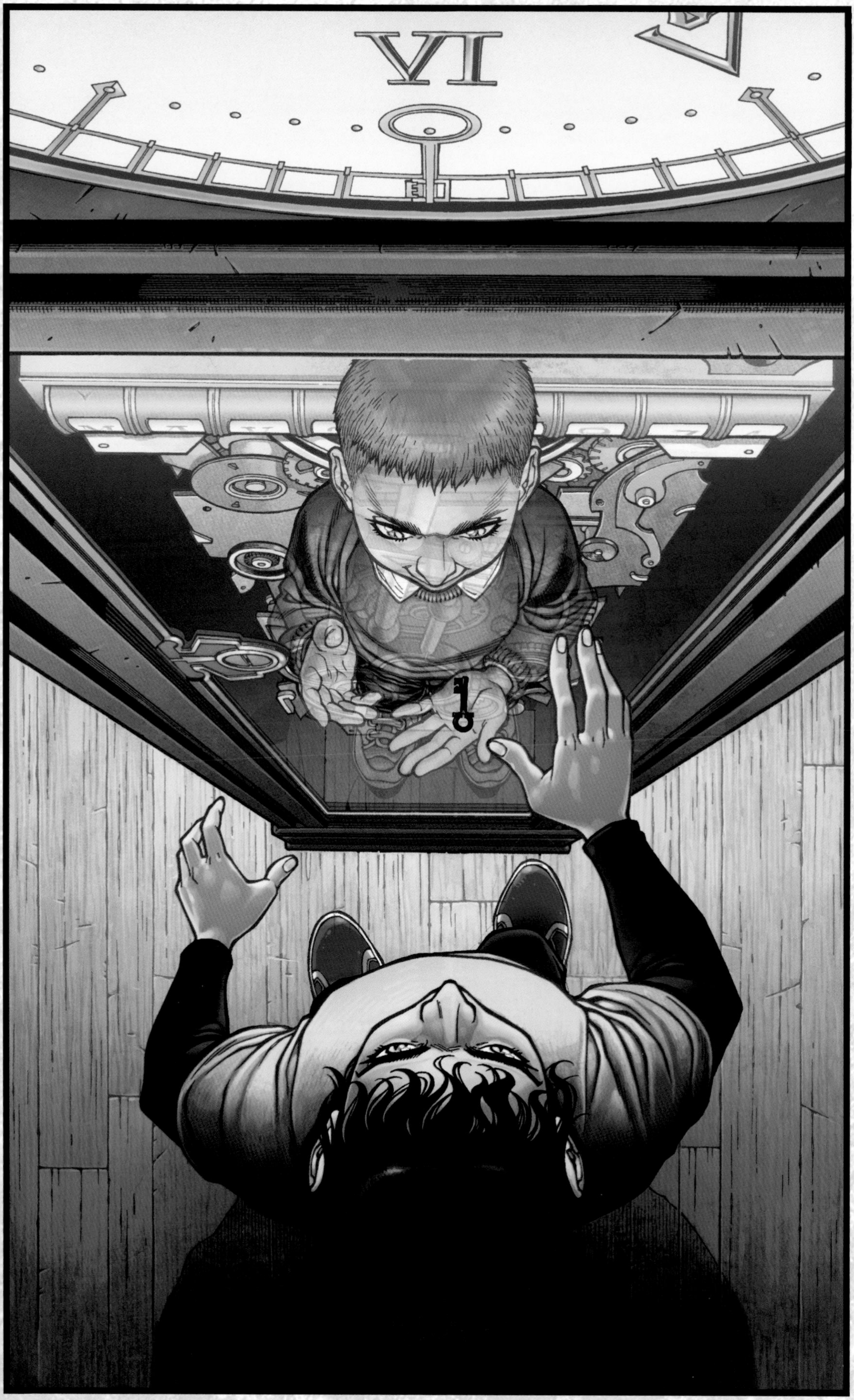

11

- CLOCKWORKS -
Chapter Four

THE WHISPERING IRON

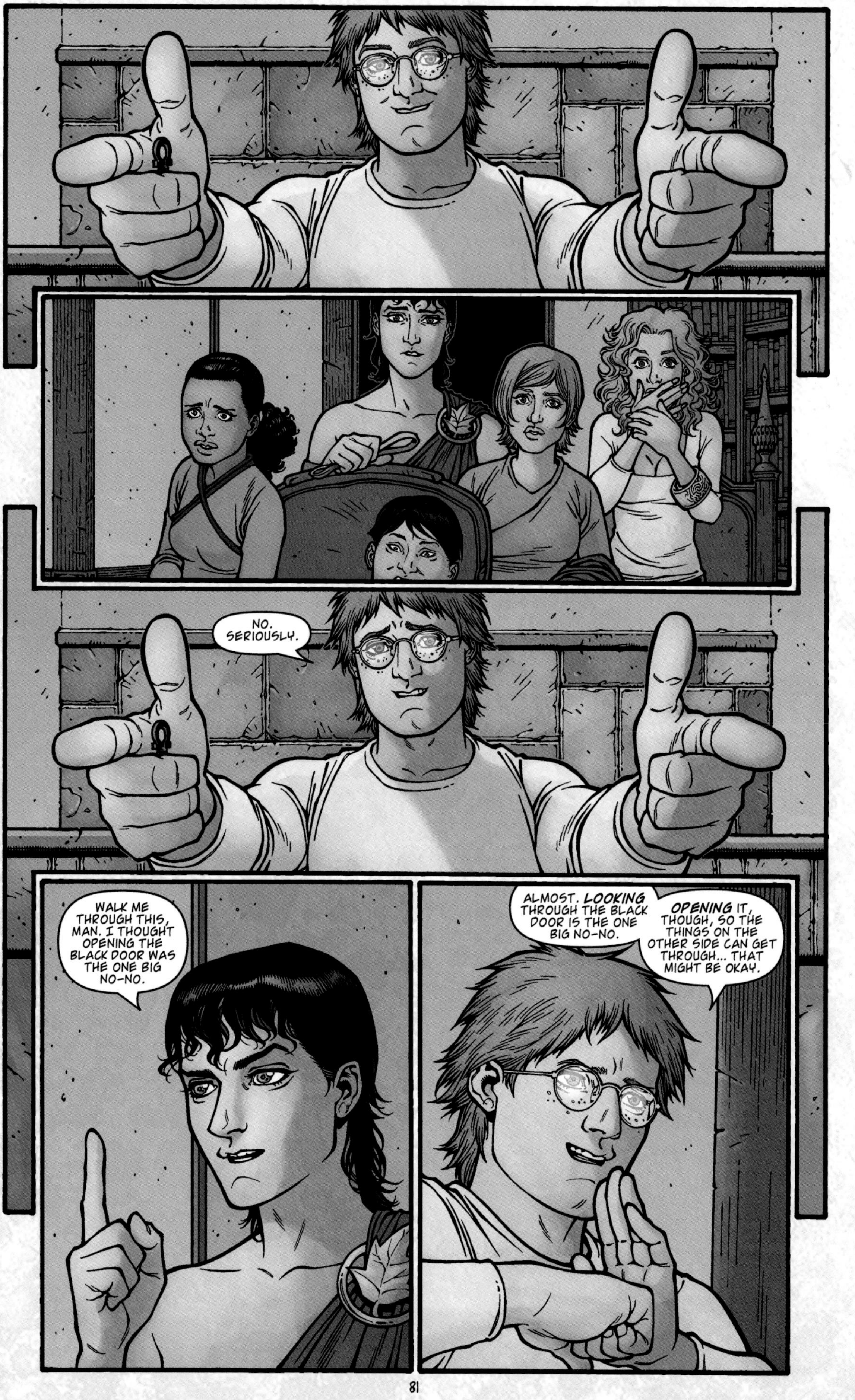
NO. SERIOUSLY.
WALK ME THROUGH THIS, MAN. I THOUGHT OPENING THE BLACK DOOR WAS THE ONE BIG NO-NO.
ALMOST. **LOOKING** THROUGH THE BLACK DOOR IS THE ONE BIG NO-NO.
OPENING IT, THOUGH, SO THE THINGS ON THE OTHER SIDE CAN GET THROUGH... THAT MIGHT BE OKAY.

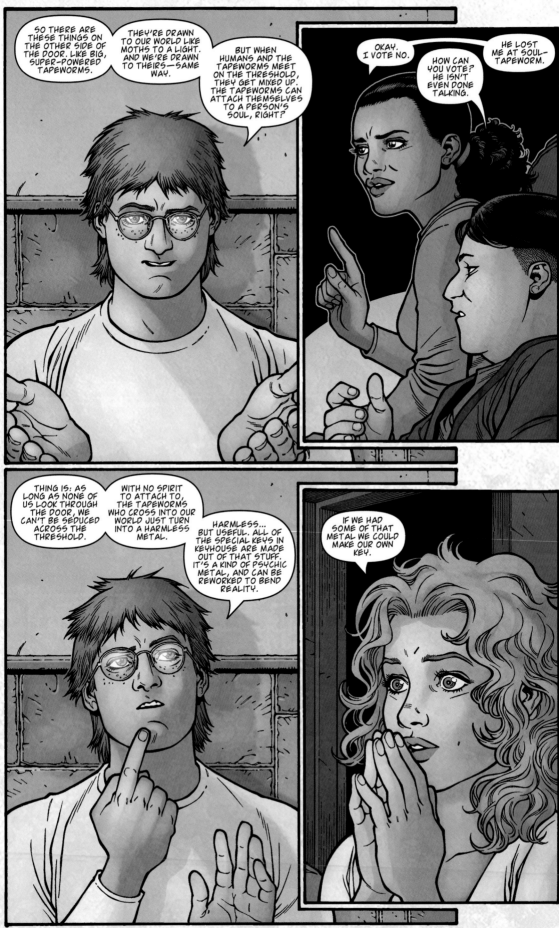

SO THERE ARE THESE THINGS ON THE OTHER SIDE OF THE DOOR. LIKE BIG, SUPER-POWERED TAPEWORMS.

THEY'RE DRAWN TO OUR WORLD LIKE MOTHS TO A LIGHT. AND WE'RE DRAWN TO THEIRS—SAME WAY.

BUT WHEN HUMANS AND THE TAPEWORMS MEET ON THE THRESHOLD, THEY GET MIXED UP. THE TAPEWORMS CAN ATTACH THEMSELVES TO A PERSON'S SOUL, RIGHT?

OKAY. I VOTE NO.

HOW CAN YOU VOTE? HE ISN'T EVEN DONE TALKING.

HE LOST ME AT SOUL-TAPEWORM.

THING IS: AS LONG AS NONE OF US LOOK THROUGH THE DOOR, WE CAN'T BE SEDUCED ACROSS THE THRESHOLD.

WITH NO SPIRIT TO ATTACH TO, THE TAPEWORMS WHO CROSS INTO OUR WORLD JUST TURN INTO A HARMLESS METAL.

HARMLESS... BUT USEFUL. ALL OF THE SPECIAL KEYS IN KEYHOUSE ARE MADE OUT OF THAT STUFF. IT'S A KIND OF PSYCHIC METAL, AND CAN BE REWORKED TO BEND REALITY.

IF WE HAD SOME OF THAT METAL WE COULD MAKE OUR OWN KEY.

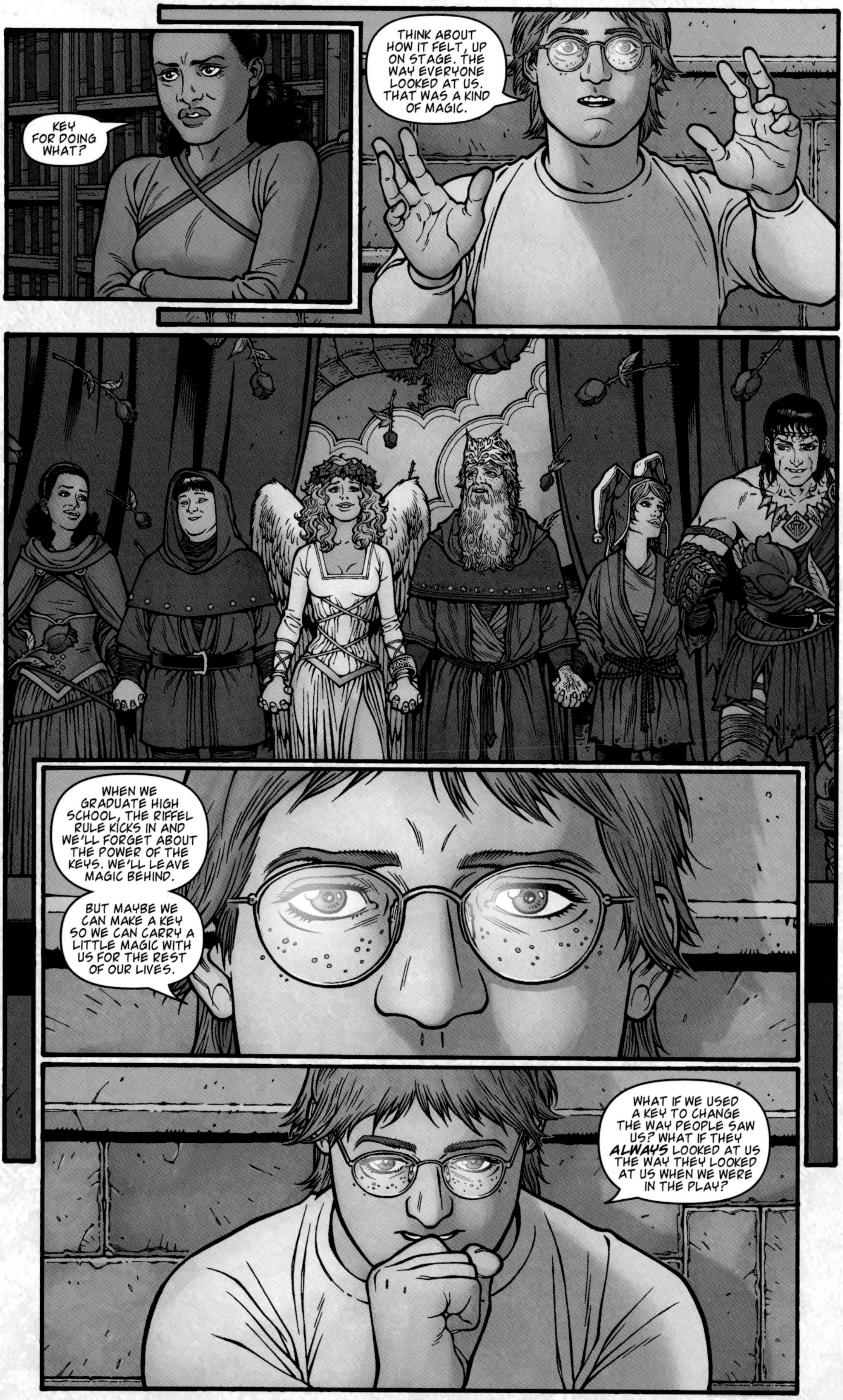
KEY FOR DOING WHAT?
THINK ABOUT HOW IT FELT, UP ON STAGE. THE WAY EVERYONE LOOKED AT US. THAT WAS A KIND OF MAGIC.
WHEN WE GRADUATE HIGH SCHOOL, THE RIFFEL RULE KICKS IN AND WE'LL FORGET ABOUT THE POWER OF THE KEYS. WE'LL LEAVE MAGIC BEHIND.
BUT MAYBE WE CAN MAKE A KEY SO WE CAN CARRY A LITTLE MAGIC WITH US FOR THE REST OF OUR LIVES.
WHAT IF WE USED A KEY TO CHANGE THE WAY PEOPLE SAW US? WHAT IF THEY ALWAYS LOOKED AT US THE WAY THEY LOOKED AT US WHEN WE WERE IN THE PLAY?

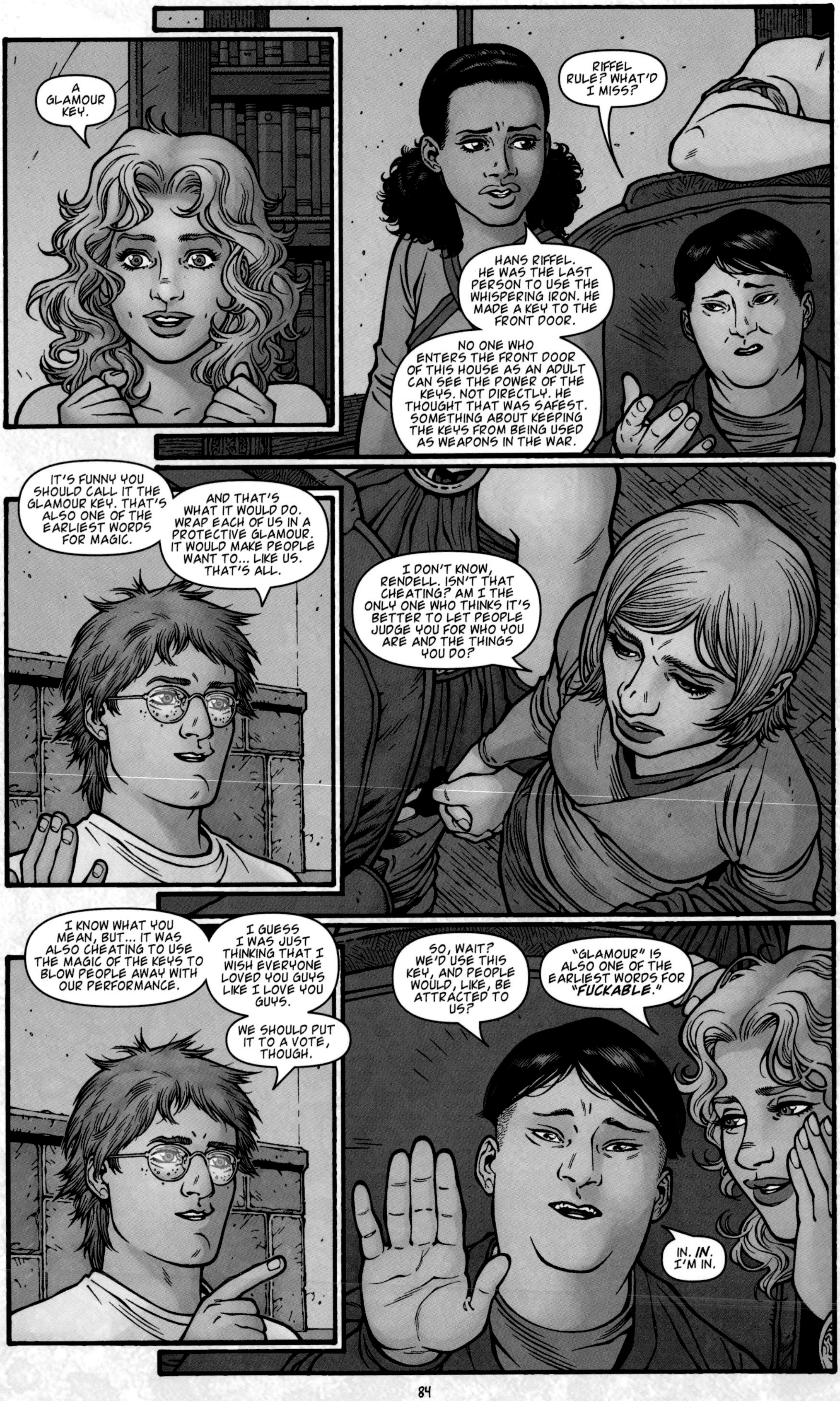
A GLAMOUR KEY.
RIFFEL RULE? WHAT'D I MISS?
HANS RIFFEL. HE WAS THE LAST PERSON TO USE THE WHISPERING IRON. HE MADE A KEY TO THE FRONT DOOR.
NO ONE WHO ENTERS THE FRONT DOOR OF THIS HOUSE AS AN ADULT CAN SEE THE POWER OF THE KEYS. NOT DIRECTLY. HE THOUGHT THAT WAS SAFEST. SOMETHING ABOUT KEEPING THE KEYS FROM BEING USED AS WEAPONS IN THE WAR.
IT'S FUNNY YOU SHOULD CALL IT THE GLAMOUR KEY. THAT'S ALSO ONE OF THE EARLIEST WORDS FOR MAGIC.
AND THAT'S WHAT IT WOULD DO. WRAP EACH OF US IN A PROTECTIVE GLAMOUR. IT WOULD MAKE PEOPLE WANT TO... LIKE US. THAT'S ALL.
I DON'T KNOW, RENDELL. ISN'T THAT CHEATING? AM I THE ONLY ONE WHO THINKS IT'S BETTER TO LET PEOPLE JUDGE YOU FOR WHO YOU ARE AND THE THINGS YOU DO?
I KNOW WHAT YOU MEAN, BUT... IT WAS ALSO CHEATING TO USE THE MAGIC OF THE KEYS TO BLOW PEOPLE AWAY WITH OUR PERFORMANCE.
I GUESS I WAS JUST THINKING THAT I WISH EVERYONE LOVED YOU GUYS LIKE I LOVE YOU GUYS.
WE SHOULD PUT IT TO A VOTE, THOUGH.
SO, WAIT? WE'D USE THIS KEY, AND PEOPLE WOULD, LIKE, BE ATTRACTED TO US?
"GLAMOUR" IS ALSO ONE OF THE EARLIEST WORDS FOR *"FUCKABLE."*
IN. *IN.* I'M IN.

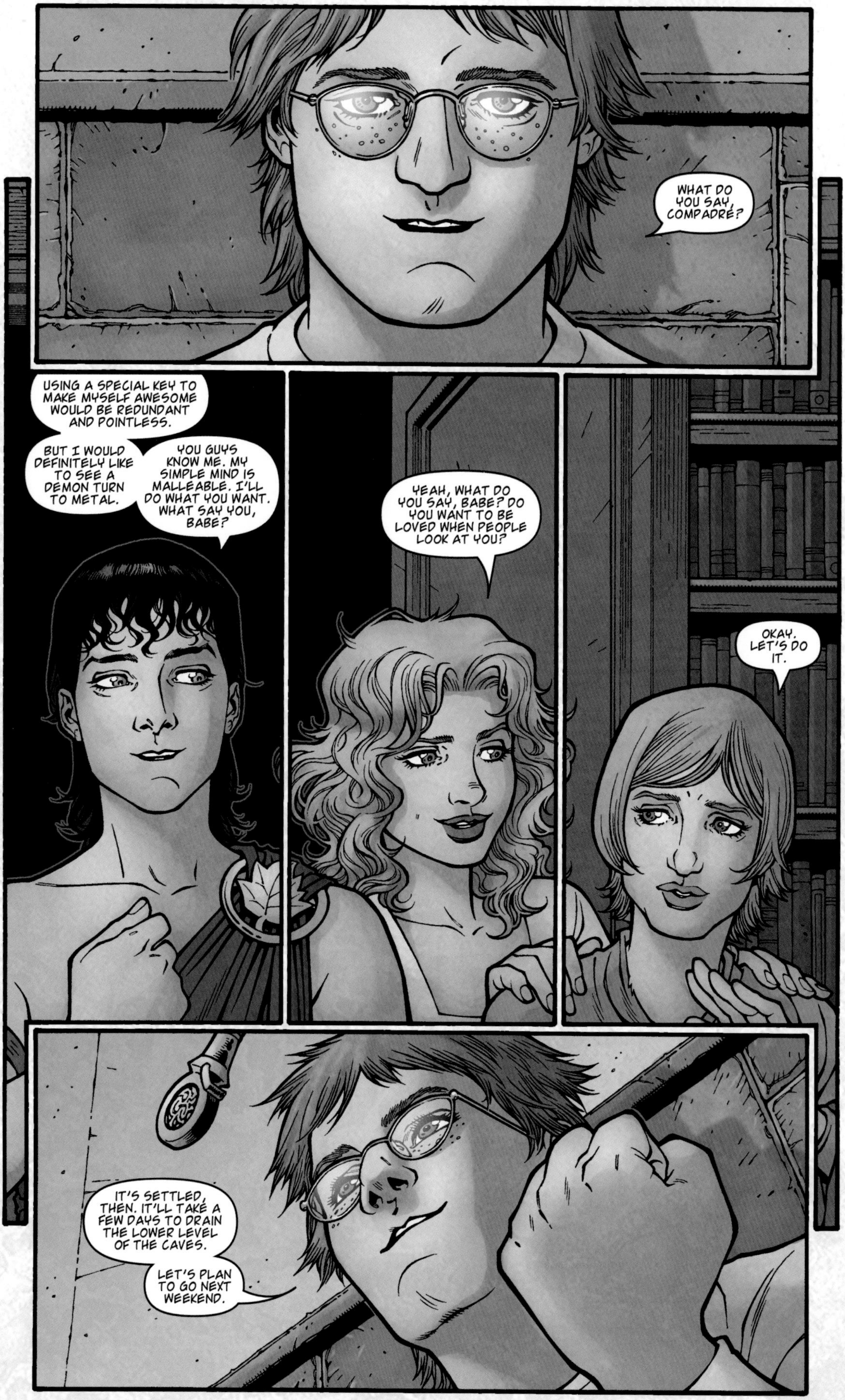
WHAT DO YOU SAY, COMPADRÉ?
USING A SPECIAL KEY TO MAKE MYSELF AWESOME WOULD BE REDUNDANT AND POINTLESS.
BUT I WOULD DEFINITELY LIKE TO SEE A DEMON TURN TO METAL.
YOU GUYS KNOW ME. MY SIMPLE MIND IS MALLEABLE. I'LL DO WHAT YOU WANT. WHAT SAY YOU, BABE?
YEAH, WHAT DO YOU SAY, BABE? DO YOU WANT TO BE LOVED WHEN PEOPLE LOOK AT YOU?
OKAY. LET'S DO IT.
IT'S SETTLED, THEN. IT'LL TAKE A FEW DAYS TO DRAIN THE LOWER LEVEL OF THE CAVES.
LET'S PLAN TO GO NEXT WEEKEND.

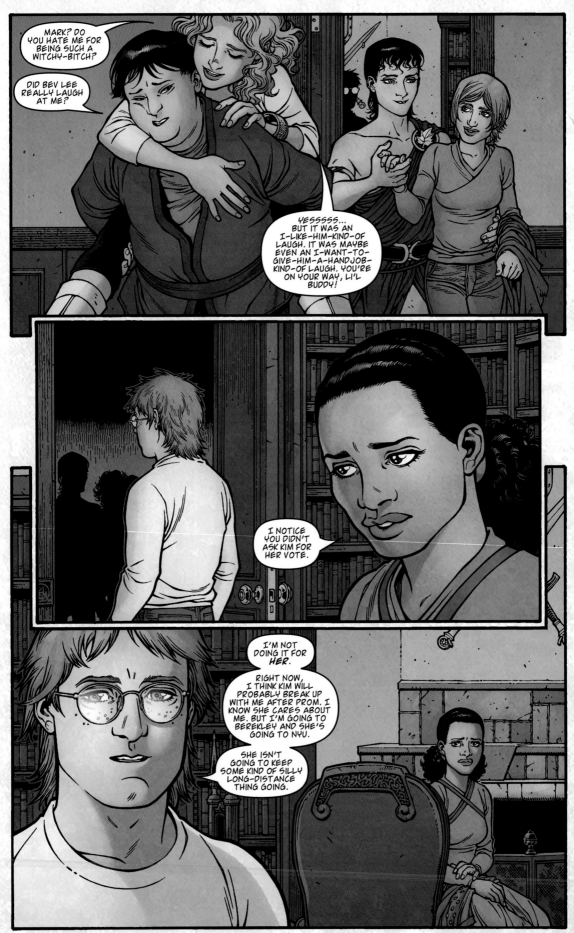

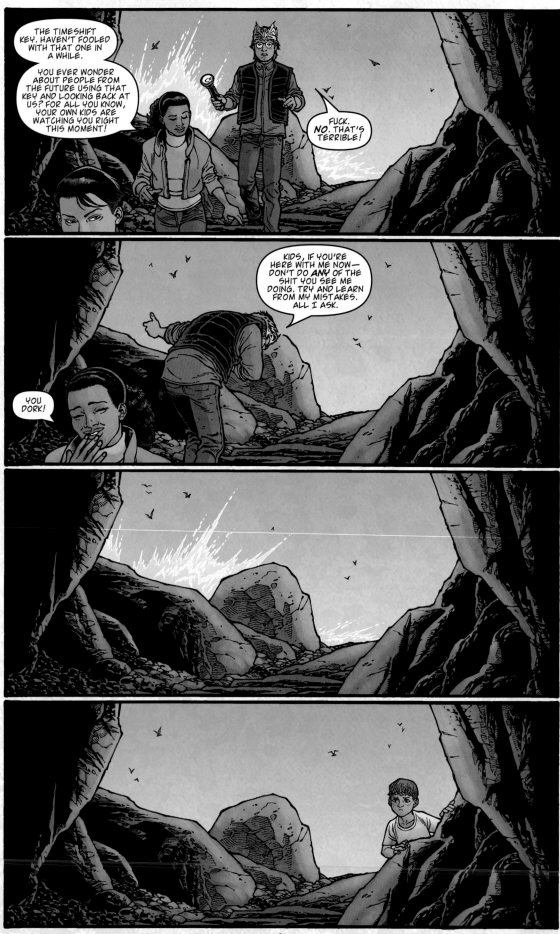

GIVE THE LITTLE GUY A BREAK. HE'S CURIOUS.

HE'S GOING TO FUCK THINGS UP. IT'S WHAT HE ALWAYS DOES!

I GOT THIS. CHILL.

TAKE IT FROM YOUR BUDDY, DODGE. IT WOULDN'T BE FUN IF SOMETHING HAPPENED TO YOU. HEAD ON BACK, OKAY?

OH, AND HEY, IF ANYONE ASKS WHERE WE WENT, FORGET YOU SAW US HERE, OKAY?

BUT WHAT ARE YOU DOING? AT LEAST TELL ME THAT!

IF YOU DON'T WANT ME TO TELL DAD YOU GUYS WENT IN THE CAVE, YOU NEED TO AT LEAST SAY WHAT YOU'RE DOING DOWN THERE.

I'LL RUN AND GO GET DAD RIGHT NOW.

NOW DARN IT, KID, THAT'S JUST NOT FAIR.

TELL. TELL AND I PROMISE— I *PROMISE*—I WON'T WALK BACK DOWN THOSE STEPS AFTER YOU.

YOU MAKE A PROMISE, YOU HAVE TO KEEP IT, NO MATTER WHAT. THAT'S HOW WE CAN TELL THE BAD GUYS FROM THE GOOD GUYS.

THE GOOD GUYS *ALWAYS* KEEP THEIR PROMISES.

OKAY. BUT YOU LISTEN UP, BUDDY. PROMISES ARE *IMPORTANT*.

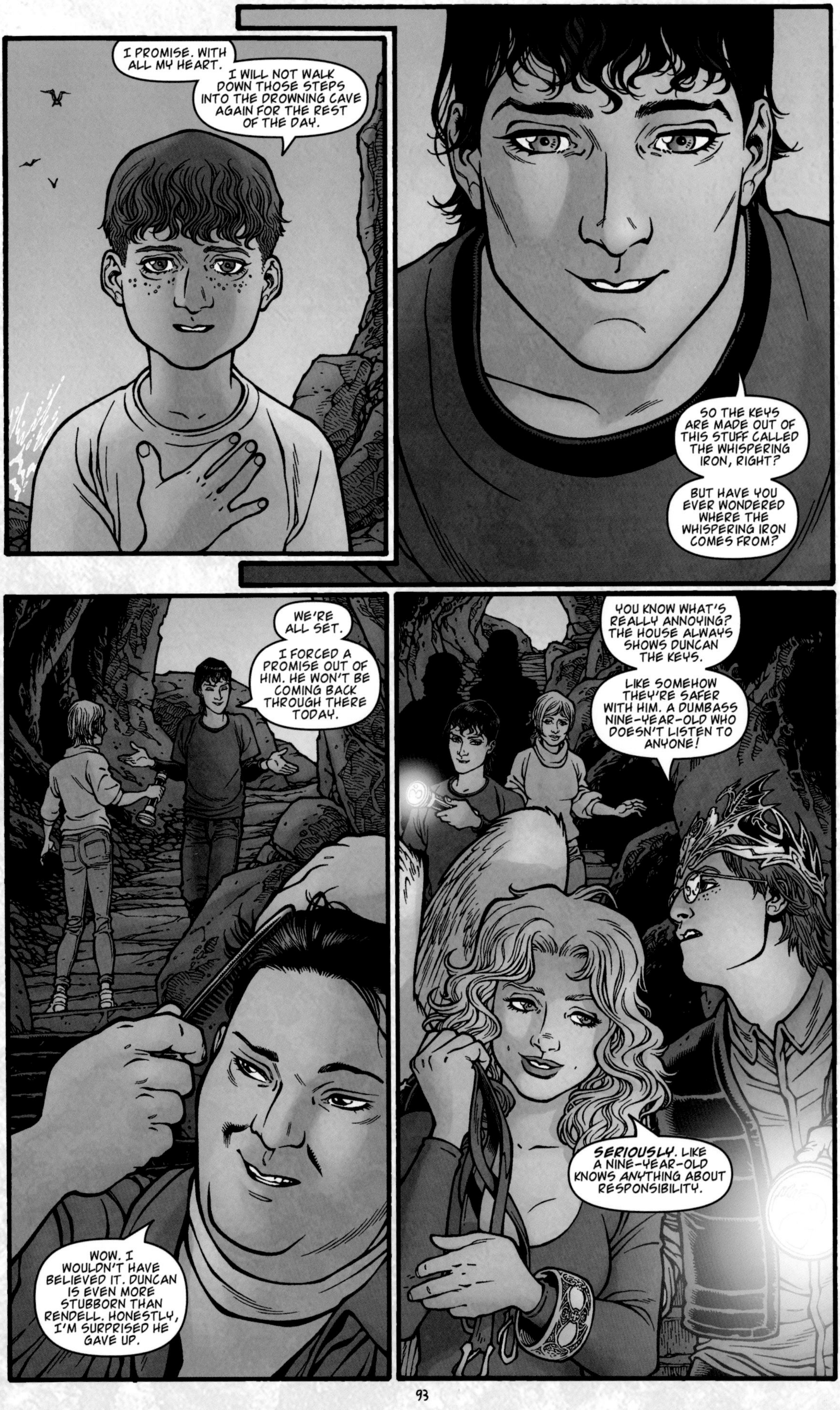
I PROMISE. WITH ALL MY HEART.
I WILL NOT WALK DOWN THOSE STEPS INTO THE DROWNING CAVE AGAIN FOR THE REST OF THE DAY.
SO THE KEYS ARE MADE OUT OF THIS STUFF CALLED THE WHISPERING IRON, RIGHT?
BUT HAVE YOU EVER WONDERED WHERE THE WHISPERING IRON COMES FROM?
WE'RE ALL SET.
I FORCED A PROMISE OUT OF HIM. HE WON'T BE COMING BACK THROUGH THERE TODAY.
WOW. I WOULDN'T HAVE BELIEVED IT. DUNCAN IS EVEN MORE STUBBORN THAN RENDELL. HONESTLY, I'M SURPRISED HE GAVE UP.
YOU KNOW WHAT'S REALLY ANNOYING? THE HOUSE ALWAYS SHOWS DUNCAN THE KEYS.
LIKE SOMEHOW THEY'RE SAFER WITH HIM. A DUMBASS NINE-YEAR-OLD WHO DOESN'T LISTEN TO ANYONE!
SERIOUSLY. LIKE A NINE-YEAR-OLD KNOWS ANYTHING ABOUT RESPONSIBILITY.

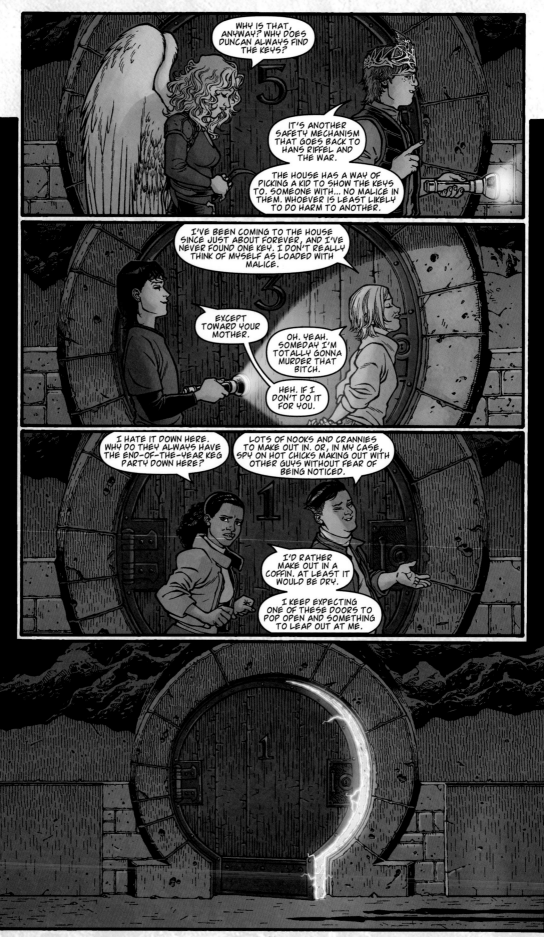

WHY IS THAT, ANYWAY? WHY DOES DUNCAN ALWAYS FIND THE KEYS?

IT'S ANOTHER SAFETY MECHANISM THAT GOES BACK TO HANS RIFFEL AND THE WAR.

THE HOUSE HAS A WAY OF PICKING A KID TO SHOW THE KEYS TO. SOMEONE WITH... NO MALICE IN THEM. WHOEVER IS LEAST LIKELY TO DO HARM TO ANOTHER.

I'VE BEEN COMING TO THE HOUSE SINCE JUST ABOUT FOREVER, AND I'VE NEVER FOUND ONE KEY. I DON'T REALLY THINK OF MYSELF AS LOADED WITH MALICE.

EXCEPT TOWARD YOUR MOTHER.

OH. YEAH. SOMEDAY I'M TOTALLY GONNA MURDER THAT BITCH.

HEH. IF I DON'T DO IT FOR YOU.

I HATE IT DOWN HERE. WHY DO THEY ALWAYS HAVE THE END-OF-THE-YEAR KEG PARTY DOWN HERE?

LOTS OF NOOKS AND CRANNIES TO MAKE OUT IN. OR, IN MY CASE, SPY ON HOT CHICKS MAKING OUT WITH OTHER GUYS WITHOUT FEAR OF BEING NOTICED.

I'D RATHER MAKE OUT IN A COFFIN. AT LEAST IT WOULD BE DRY.

I KEEP EXPECTING ONE OF THESE DOORS TO POP OPEN AND SOMETHING TO LEAP OUT AT ME.

ONE WAY OR ANOTHER—THIS HAS BEEN THE BEST YEAR OF MY LIFE. BECAUSE OF YOU GUYS.

HEY—STICK "DODGE" IN THERE AS MY MIDDLE NAME. FAR AS I'M CONCERNED, THAT'S MY REAL NAME.

BECAUSE IT'S YOUR NAME FOR ME.

KEEPERS OF THE KEYS—
TAMERS OF THE TEMPEST

RENDELL LOCKE

ERIN VOSS

KIM TOPHER

ELLIE WHEDON

MARK CHO

LUKE "DODGE" CARAVAGGIO

FRIENDS FOREVER

1988

WHY'D YOU PUT MY NAME AFTER RENDELL'S? I MEAN, HE'S IN LOVE WITH KIM, RIGHT?

I WASN'T THINKING ABOUT WHO HE'S IN LOVE WITH.

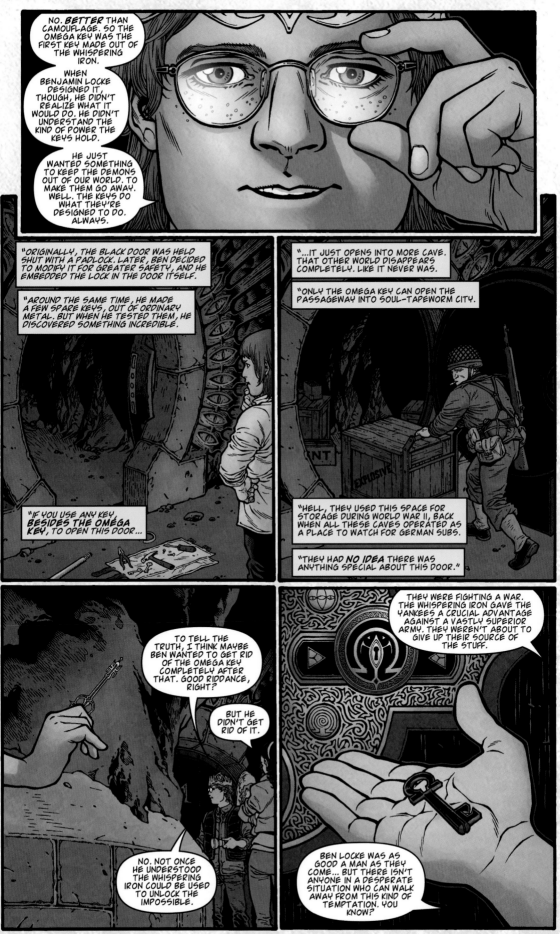

NO. *BETTER* THAN CAMOUFLAGE. SO THE OMEGA KEY WAS THE FIRST KEY MADE OUT OF THE WHISPERING IRON.

WHEN BENJAMIN LOCKE DESIGNED IT, THOUGH, HE DIDN'T REALIZE WHAT IT WOULD DO. HE DIDN'T UNDERSTAND THE KIND OF POWER THE KEYS HOLD.

HE JUST WANTED SOMETHING TO KEEP THE DEMONS OUT OF OUR WORLD. TO MAKE THEM GO AWAY. WELL. THE KEYS DO WHAT THEY'RE DESIGNED TO DO. ALWAYS.

"ORIGINALLY, THE BLACK DOOR WAS HELD SHUT WITH A PADLOCK. LATER, BEN DECIDED TO MODIFY IT FOR GREATER SAFETY, AND HE EMBEDDED THE LOCK IN THE DOOR ITSELF.

"AROUND THE SAME TIME, HE MADE A FEW SPARE KEYS, OUT OF ORDINARY METAL. BUT WHEN HE TESTED THEM, HE DISCOVERED SOMETHING INCREDIBLE.

"IF YOU USE ANY KEY, *BESIDES THE OMEGA KEY*, TO OPEN THIS DOOR...

"...IT JUST OPENS INTO MORE CAVE. THAT OTHER WORLD DISAPPEARS COMPLETELY. LIKE IT NEVER WAS.

"ONLY THE OMEGA KEY CAN OPEN THE PASSAGEWAY INTO SOUL-TAPEWORM CITY.

"HELL, THEY USED THIS SPACE FOR STORAGE DURING WORLD WAR II, BACK WHEN ALL THESE CAVES OPERATED AS A PLACE TO WATCH FOR GERMAN SUBS.

"THEY HAD *NO IDEA* THERE WAS ANYTHING SPECIAL ABOUT THIS DOOR."

TO TELL THE TRUTH, I THINK MAYBE BEN WANTED TO GET RID OF THE OMEGA KEY COMPLETELY AFTER THAT. GOOD RIDDANCE, RIGHT?

BUT HE DIDN'T GET RID OF IT.

NO. NOT ONCE HE UNDERSTOOD THE WHISPERING IRON COULD BE USED TO UNLOCK THE IMPOSSIBLE.

THEY WERE FIGHTING A WAR. THE WHISPERING IRON GAVE THE YANKEES A CRUCIAL ADVANTAGE AGAINST A VASTLY SUPERIOR ARMY. THEY WEREN'T ABOUT TO GIVE UP THEIR SOURCE OF THE STUFF.

BEN LOCKE WAS AS GOOD A MAN AS THEY COME... BUT THERE ISN'T ANYONE IN A DESPERATE SITUATION WHO CAN WALK AWAY FROM THIS KIND OF TEMPTATION. YOU KNOW?

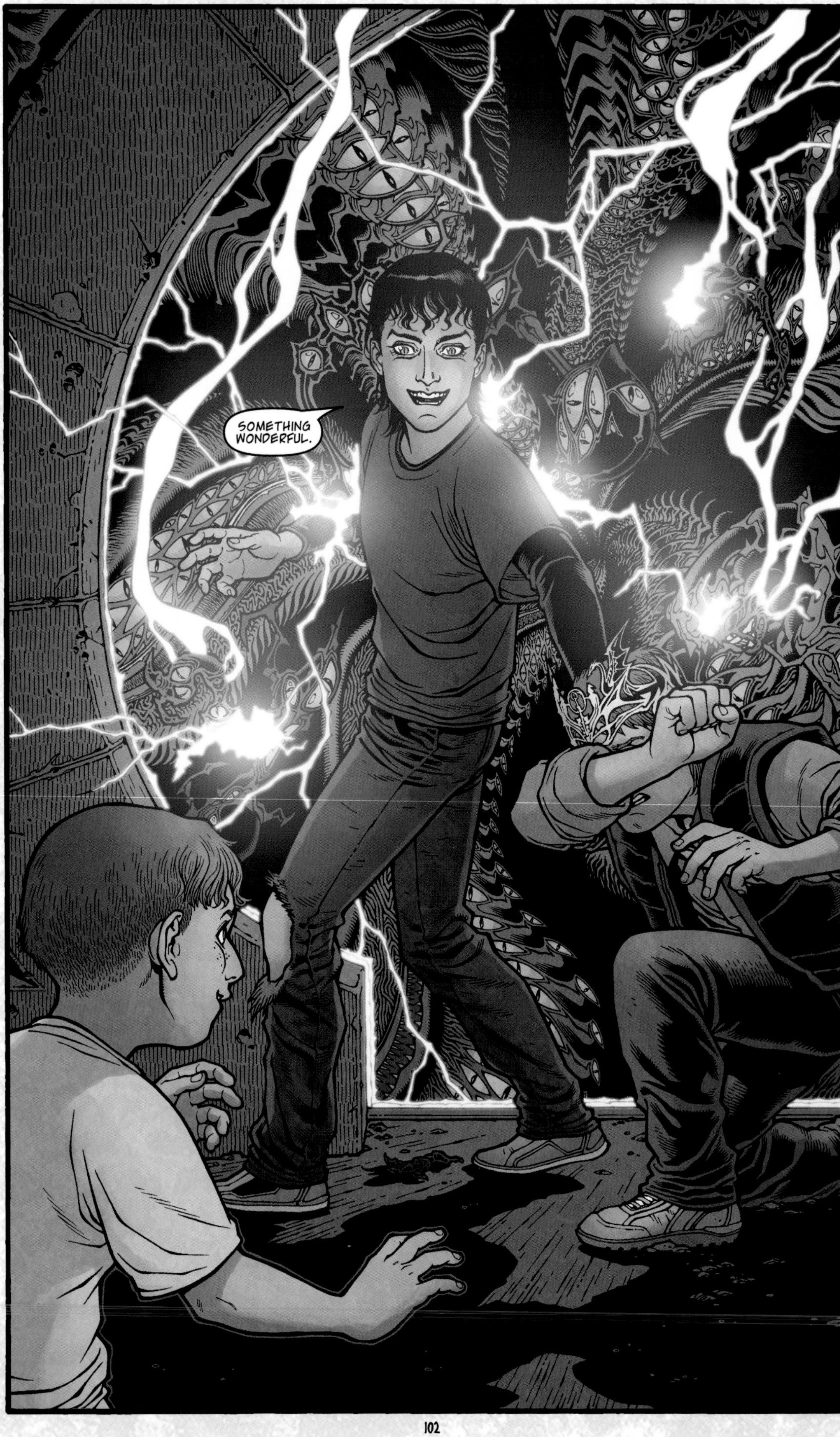
SOMETHING WONDERFUL.

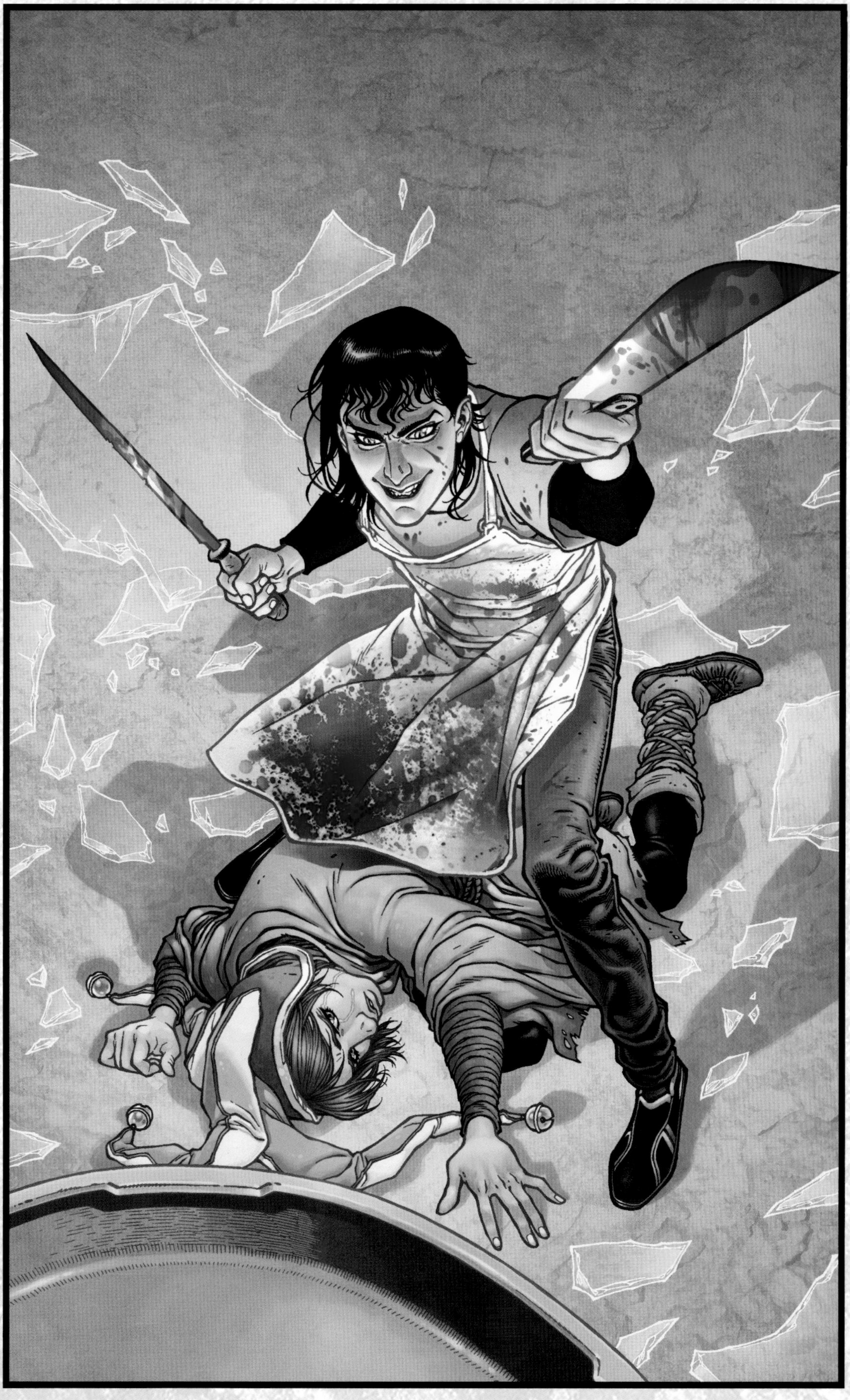

- CLOCKWORKS -

Chapter Five

GROWN~UPS

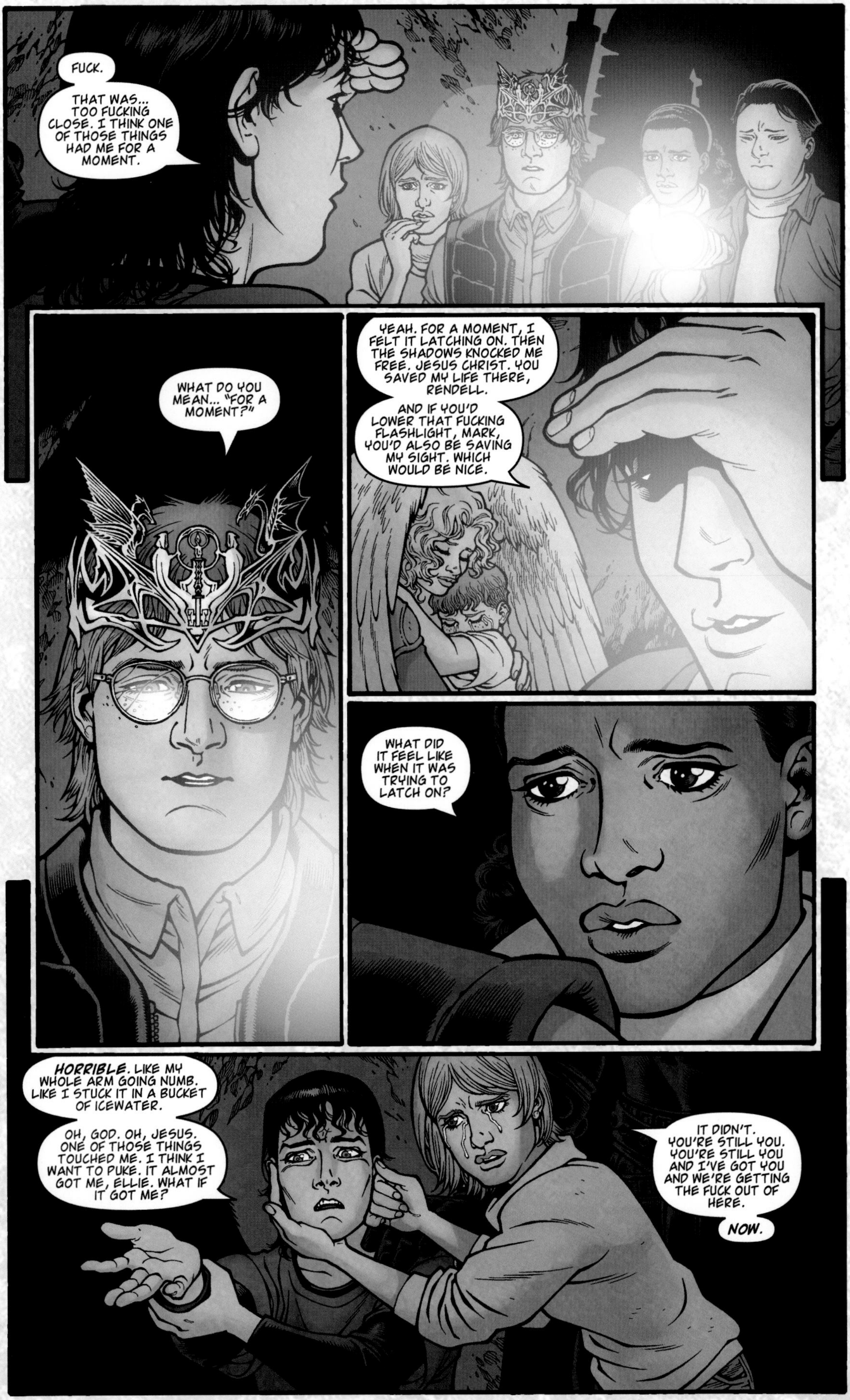
FUCK.
THAT WAS... TOO FUCKING CLOSE. I THINK ONE OF THOSE THINGS HAD ME FOR A MOMENT.
WHAT DO YOU MEAN... "FOR A MOMENT?"
YEAH. FOR A MOMENT, I FELT IT LATCHING ON. THEN THE SHADOWS KNOCKED ME FREE. JESUS CHRIST. YOU SAVED MY LIFE THERE, RENDELL.
AND IF YOU'D LOWER THAT FUCKING FLASHLIGHT, MARK, YOU'D ALSO BE SAVING MY SIGHT. WHICH WOULD BE NICE.
WHAT DID IT FEEL LIKE WHEN IT WAS TRYING TO LATCH ON?
HORRIBLE. LIKE MY WHOLE ARM GOING NUMB. LIKE I STUCK IT IN A BUCKET OF ICEWATER.
OH, GOD. OH, JESUS. ONE OF THOSE THINGS TOUCHED ME. I THINK I WANT TO PUKE. IT ALMOST GOT ME, ELLIE. WHAT IF IT GOT ME?
IT DIDN'T. YOU'RE STILL YOU. YOU'RE STILL YOU AND I'VE GOT YOU AND WE'RE GETTING THE FUCK OUT OF HERE.
NOW.

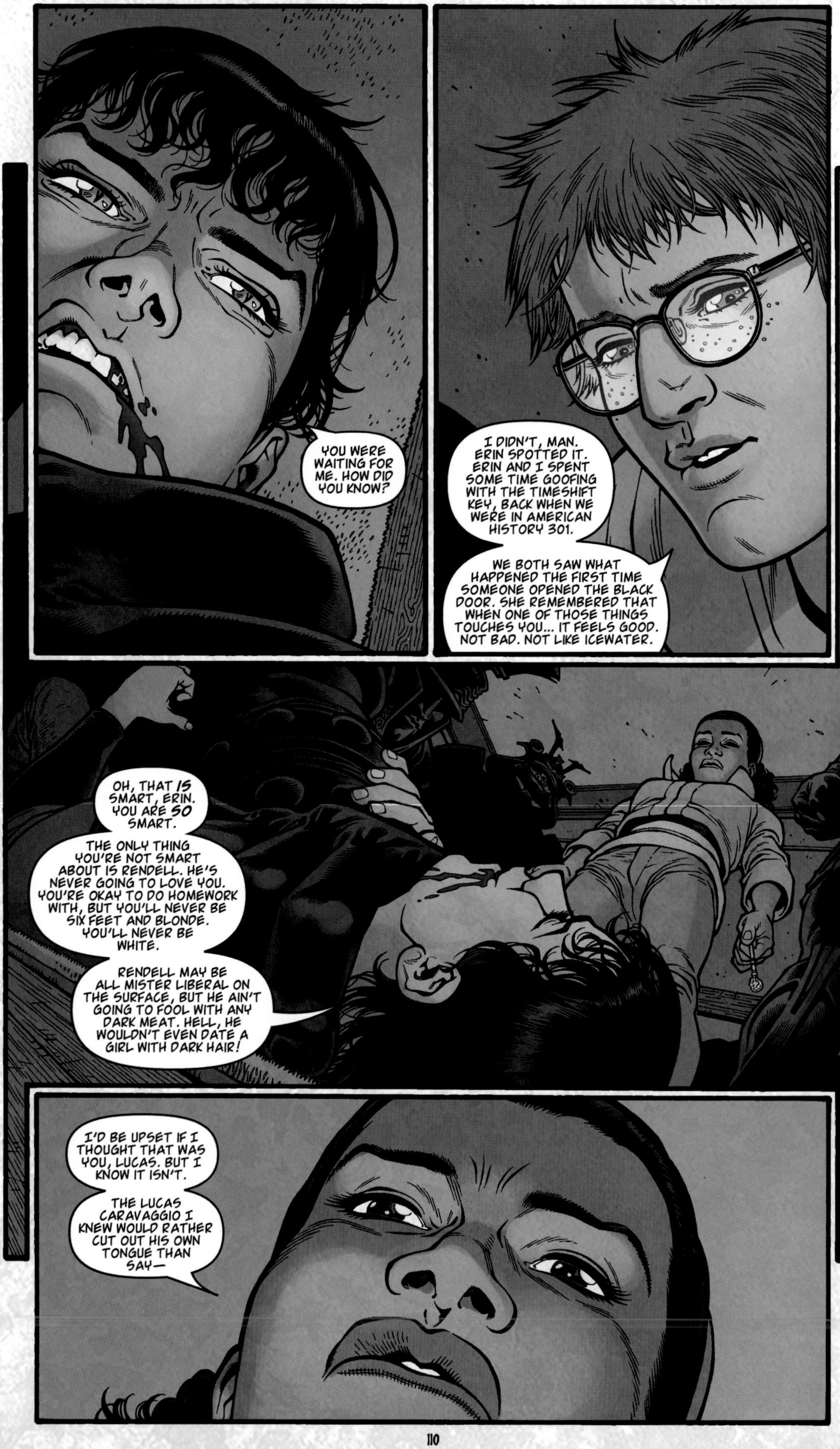

YOU WERE WAITING FOR ME. HOW DID YOU KNOW?
I DIDN'T, MAN. ERIN SPOTTED IT. ERIN AND I SPENT SOME TIME GOOFING WITH THE TIMESHIFT KEY, BACK WHEN WE WERE IN AMERICAN HISTORY 301.
WE BOTH SAW WHAT HAPPENED THE FIRST TIME SOMEONE OPENED THE BLACK DOOR. SHE REMEMBERED THAT WHEN ONE OF THOSE THINGS TOUCHES YOU... IT FEELS GOOD. NOT BAD. NOT LIKE ICEWATER.
OH, THAT IS SMART, ERIN. YOU ARE SO SMART.
THE ONLY THING YOU'RE NOT SMART ABOUT IS RENDELL. HE'S NEVER GOING TO LOVE YOU. YOU'RE OKAY TO DO HOMEWORK WITH, BUT YOU'LL NEVER BE SIX FEET AND BLONDE. YOU'LL NEVER BE WHITE.
RENDELL MAY BE ALL MISTER LIBERAL ON THE SURFACE, BUT HE AIN'T GOING TO FOOL WITH ANY DARK MEAT. HELL, HE WOULDN'T EVEN DATE A GIRL WITH DARK HAIR!
I'D BE UPSET IF I THOUGHT THAT WAS YOU, LUCAS. BUT I KNOW IT ISN'T.
THE LUCAS CARAVAGGIO I KNEW WOULD RATHER CUT OUT HIS OWN TONGUE THAN SAY—

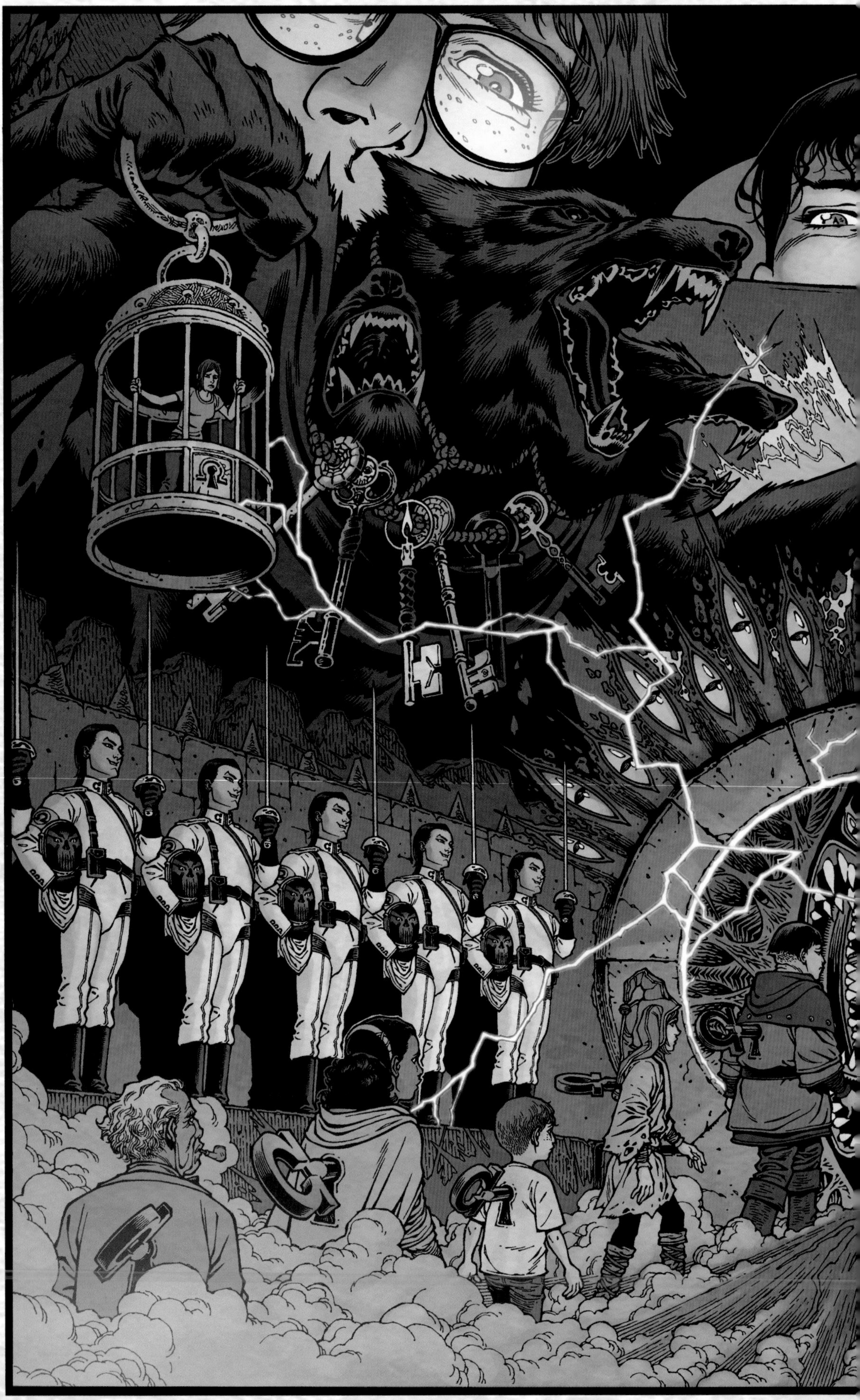

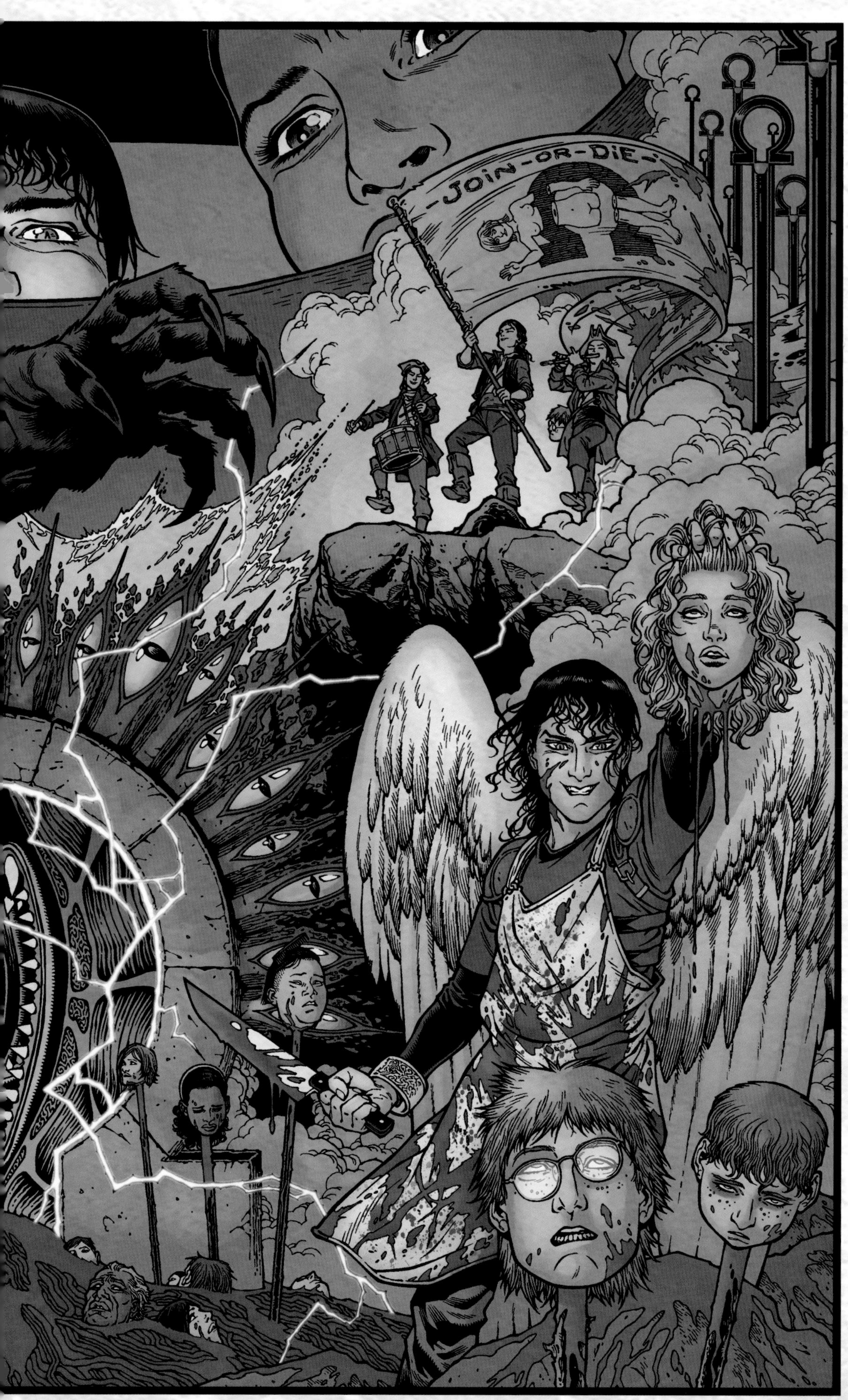
-JOIN-OR-DIE-

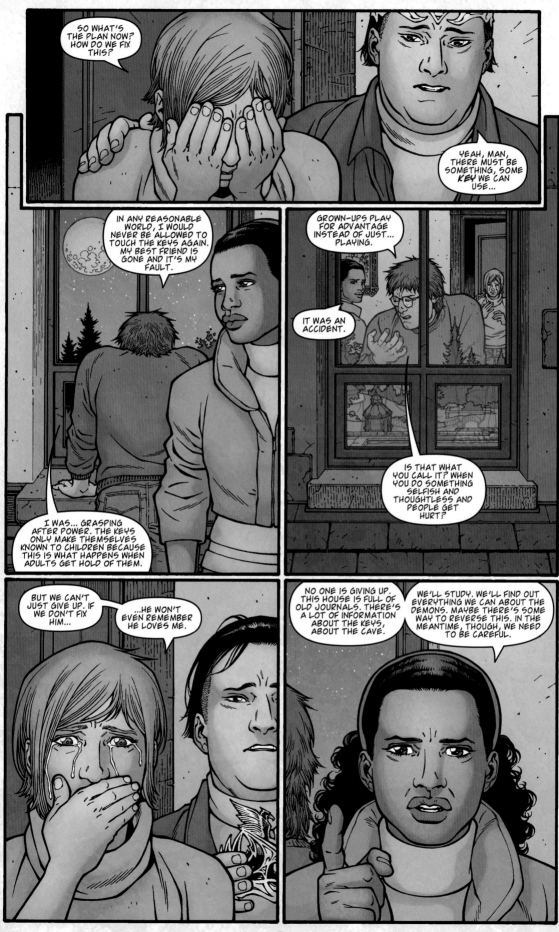

SO WHAT'S THE PLAN NOW? HOW DO WE FIX THIS?

YEAH, MAN, THERE MUST BE SOMETHING, SOME *KEY* WE CAN USE...

IN ANY REASONABLE WORLD, I WOULD NEVER BE ALLOWED TO TOUCH THE KEYS AGAIN. MY BEST FRIEND IS GONE AND IT'S MY FAULT.

I WAS... GRASPING AFTER POWER. THE KEYS ONLY MAKE THEMSELVES KNOWN TO CHILDREN BECAUSE THIS IS WHAT HAPPENS WHEN ADULTS GET HOLD OF THEM.

GROWN-UPS PLAY FOR ADVANTAGE INSTEAD OF JUST... PLAYING.

IT WAS AN ACCIDENT.

IS THAT WHAT YOU CALL IT? WHEN YOU DO SOMETHING SELFISH AND THOUGHTLESS AND PEOPLE GET HURT?

BUT WE CAN'T JUST GIVE UP. IF WE DON'T FIX HIM...

...HE WON'T EVEN REMEMBER HE LOVES ME.

NO ONE IS GIVING UP. THIS HOUSE IS FULL OF OLD JOURNALS. THERE'S A LOT OF INFORMATION ABOUT THE KEYS, ABOUT THE CAVE.

WE'LL STUDY. WE'LL FIND OUT EVERYTHING WE CAN ABOUT THE DEMONS. MAYBE THERE'S SOME WAY TO REVERSE THIS. IN THE MEANTIME, THOUGH, WE NEED TO BE CAREFUL.

WE'VE STRIPPED DODGE OF MOST OF HIS MEMORIES, BUT WE HAVE TO ASSUME HE'S STILL DANGEROUS.

EVERYONE SHOULD KEEP A KEY ON THEM AT ALL TIMES, TO PROTECT THEMSELVES FROM HIM. MARK, YOU HOLD ON TO THE CROWN. KIM, YOU'VE GOT YOUR WINGS. ELLIE—

I'M NOT GOING TO PROTECT MYSELF FROM LUKE!

I'M NOT GOING TO USE ANY KEY ON HIM, EITHER.

AW, ELLIE— ELLIE—!

WHAT WE JUST DID TO HIM IS ENOUGH. MORE THAN ENOUGH—IT WAS LIKE RAPE. IT WAS WORSE THAN RAPE.

THE KEYS, THE FUCKING KEYS—THEY MAKE ME WANT TO PUKE. ALL OF YOU MAKE ME WANT TO FUCKING PUKE!

LET HER GO, MARK. SHE'S BEEN THROUGH A LOT. SHE NEEDS TIME. AND SLEEP.

WE ALL NEED SLEEP. WE SHOULD PROBABLY CLEAR OUT. BE DONE FOR TONIGHT.

ISN'T THERE ONE MORE THING TO FIGURE OUT? WHERE ARE WE GOING TO PUT DODGE'S MEMORIES? WHERE WILL THEY BE SAFE?

I'VE GOT JUST THE PLACE.

THERE'LL EVEN BE SOMEONE TO GUARD THEM.

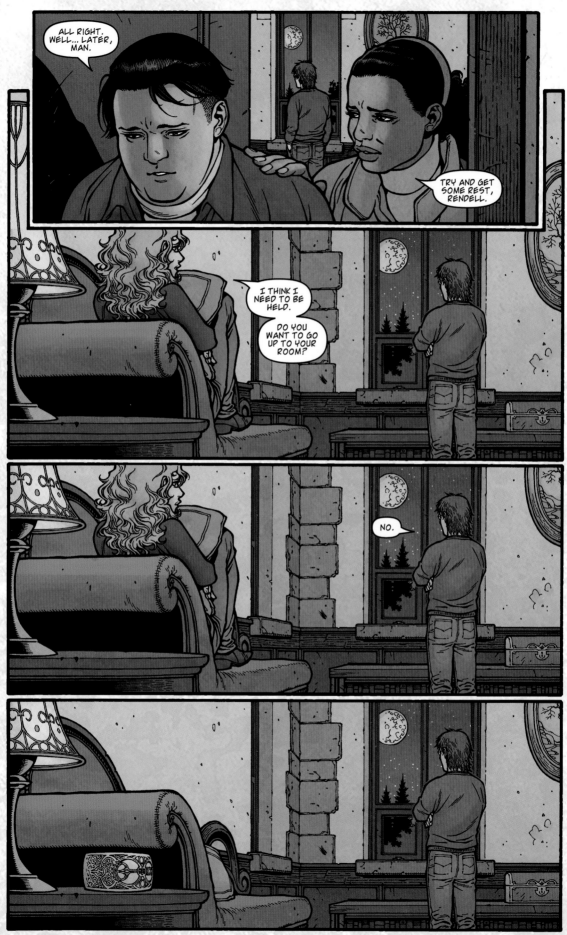

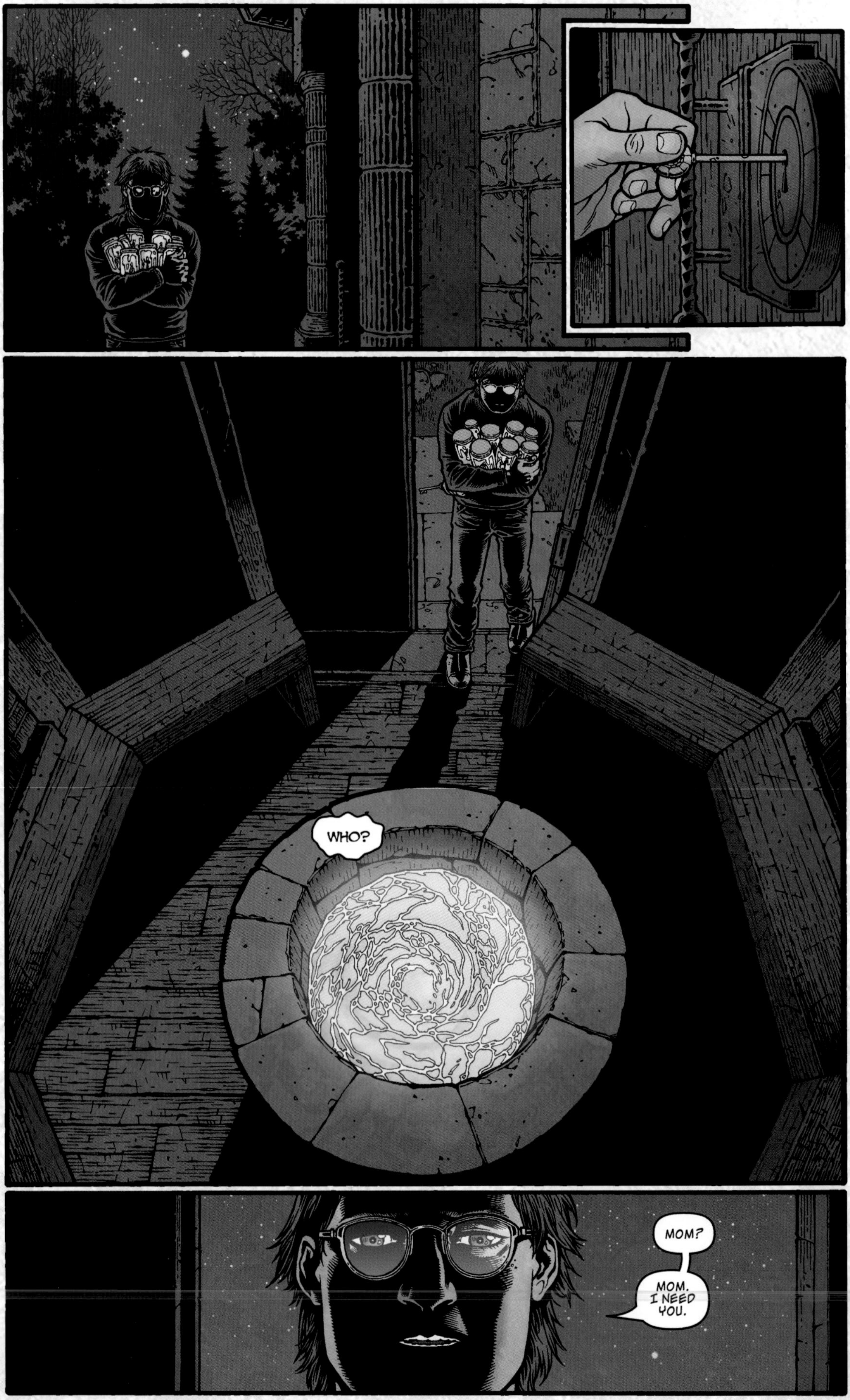
WHO?
MOM?
MOM. I NEED YOU.

LOVECRAFT SENIOR DRAMA — *THE TEMPEST*
From Left: MARK CHO, LUCAS CARAVAGGIO, ELLIE WHEDON, RENDELL LOCKE, KIM TOPHER, ...OSS, ...sor JOE RIDGEWAY - Director.

LOOK AT YOU. STOP MILKIN' IT, WHY DON'T YOU?

HE'S MOVED ON. YOU OUGHT TO MOVE ON YOUR OWN SELF. THE LITTLE DAGO IS DOIN' SOME BLONDE NOW, INN'T HE?

IS THAT HER? HIS NEW PIECE? KIM TOPHER? LITTLE MISS RICH BITCH, WHO YOU THOUGHT WAS SUCH A GOOD FRIEND?

I TOLT YOU IT WOULD COME TO GRIEF. RUNNIN' AROUND WITH THE RICH KIDS, KIDDING YOURSELF YOU COULD EVER BE ONE OF 'EM.

I TOLT YOU, YOU SHOULDA GIVEN A CHANCE TO GIL FARMINGTON, DOWN AT THE SHELL STATION. THAT'S A GUY WOULDN'T LEAVE YOU IN THE LURCH. I TOLT YOU—

YOU SURE DID TELL ME, MOM. I'M GOING FOR A RUN.

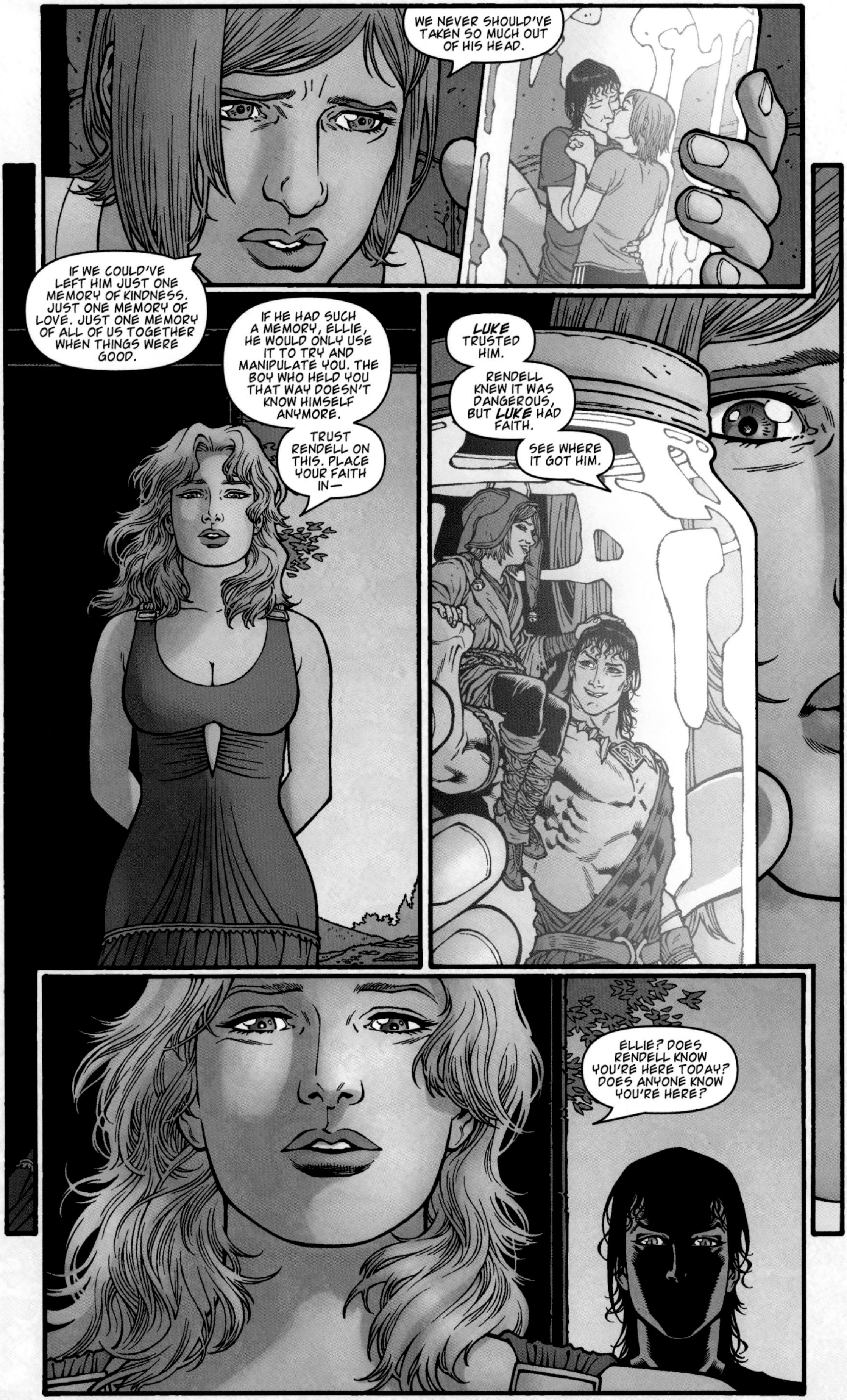
WE NEVER SHOULD'VE TAKEN SO MUCH OUT OF HIS HEAD.
IF WE COULD'VE LEFT HIM JUST ONE MEMORY OF KINDNESS. JUST ONE MEMORY OF LOVE. JUST ONE MEMORY OF ALL OF US TOGETHER WHEN THINGS WERE GOOD.
IF HE HAD SUCH A MEMORY, ELLIE, HE WOULD ONLY USE IT TO TRY AND MANIPULATE YOU. THE BOY WHO HELD YOU THAT WAY DOESN'T KNOW HIMSELF ANYMORE.
TRUST RENDELL ON THIS. PLACE YOUR FAITH IN—
LUKE TRUSTED HIM.
RENDELL KNEW IT WAS DANGEROUS, BUT LUKE HAD FAITH.
SEE WHERE IT GOT HIM.
ELLIE? DOES RENDELL KNOW YOU'RE HERE TODAY? DOES ANYONE KNOW YOU'RE HERE?

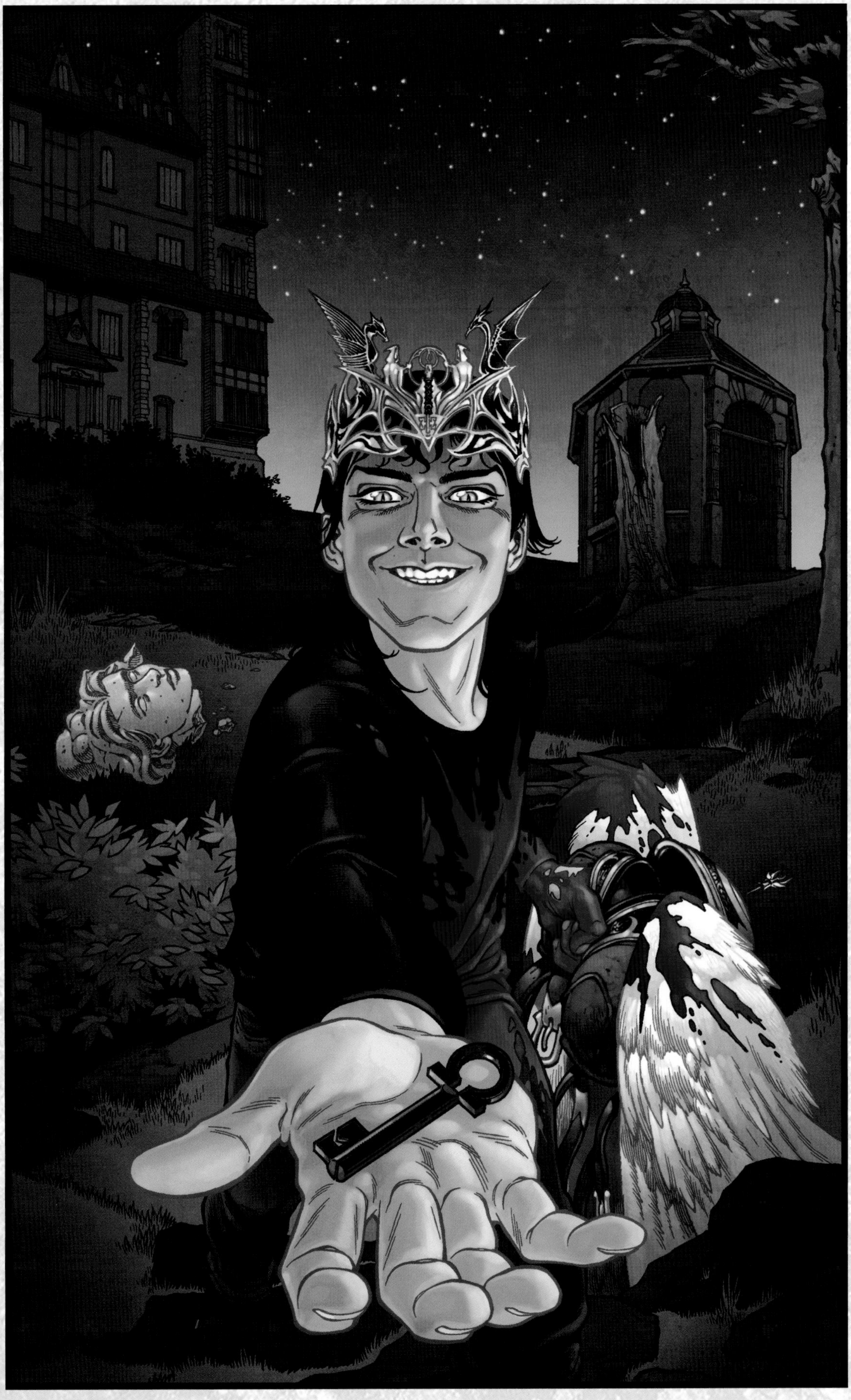

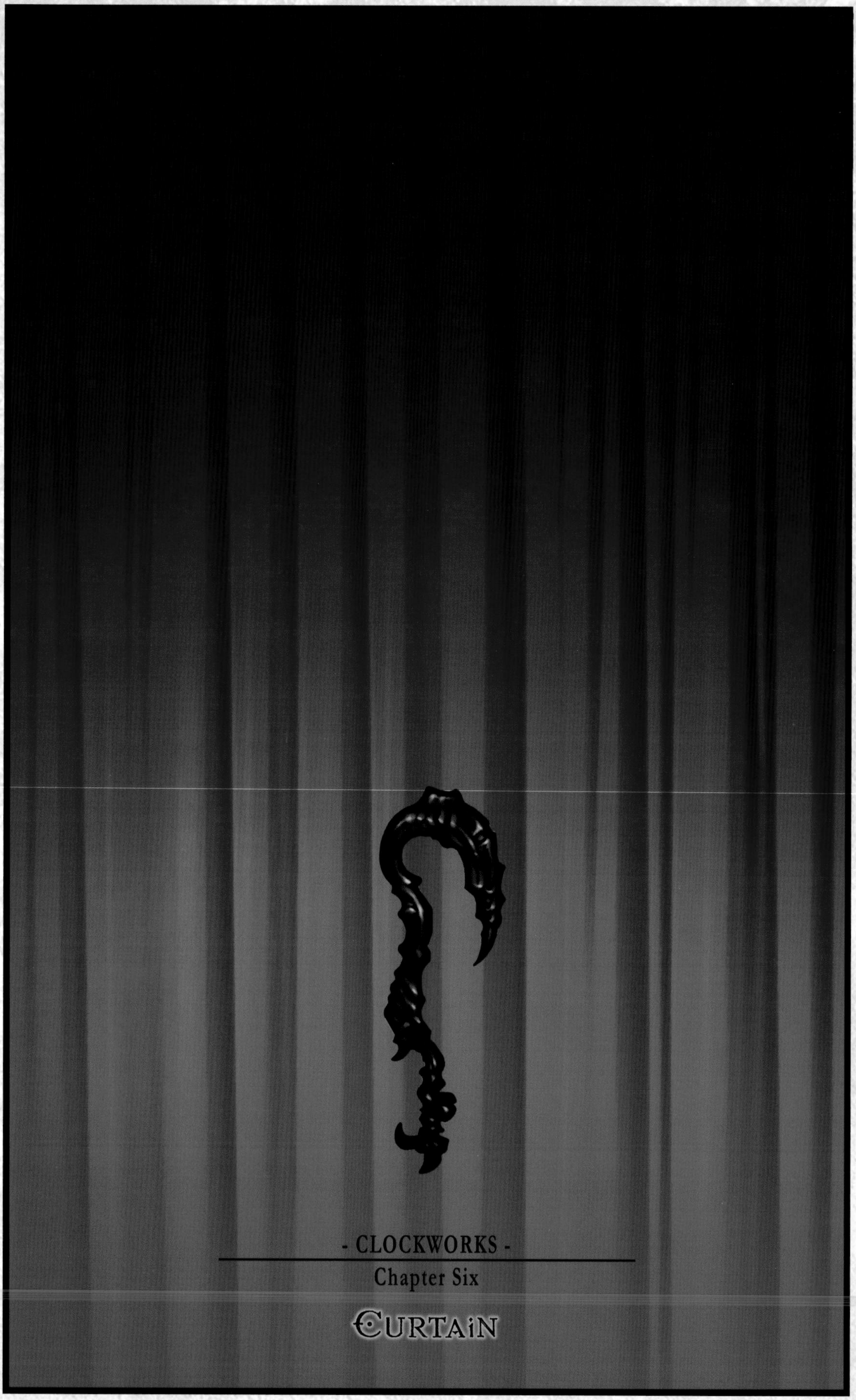
- CLOCKWORKS -
Chapter Six
CURTAIN

RUNNING.

OH. ANY IDEA WHERE?

YOU OUGHT TO LEAVE HER BE. GOIN' AROUND WITH YOU AND YOUR FRIENDS IS WHAT GOT HER SO MESSED UP. I KNEW LETTIN' HER GO TO THE ACADEMY WAS A MISTAKE. SHE'S A TOWNIE. SHE'S ALWAYS GONNA BE A TOWNIE.

ELLIE PROLLY JOGGED UP TO KEYHOUSE TO SIT AND CRY OVER THAT GREASY LITTLE NITWIT WHO DUMPED HER.

THAT'S A VERY... INTERESTING LINE OF THOUGHT ON CLASS DIVISION IN THE LOCAL COMMUNITY, MRS. WHEDON.

WELL, THANKS! SORRY TO BOTHER YOU.

LET'S SEE... SOMETHING TO WRITE WITH, PLEASE. AND TAPE. AND, I THINK—

TAKE THIS TO ELLIE'S. HIDE IT SOMEPLACE WHERE SHE'LL NEVER FIND IT... UNTIL THE DAY SHE DOES.

BE CAREFUL WITH THAT. DYING IS FINE FOR OTHER PEOPLE, BUT I DON'T THINK IT'S FOR ME. THIS IS MY RESET BUTTON IF THINGS DON'T WORK OUT IN THE CAVE.

CASE OF EMERGENCY BREAK GLASS

SAMURAI—MAKE SURE THEY KNOW WHERE WE'RE GOING.

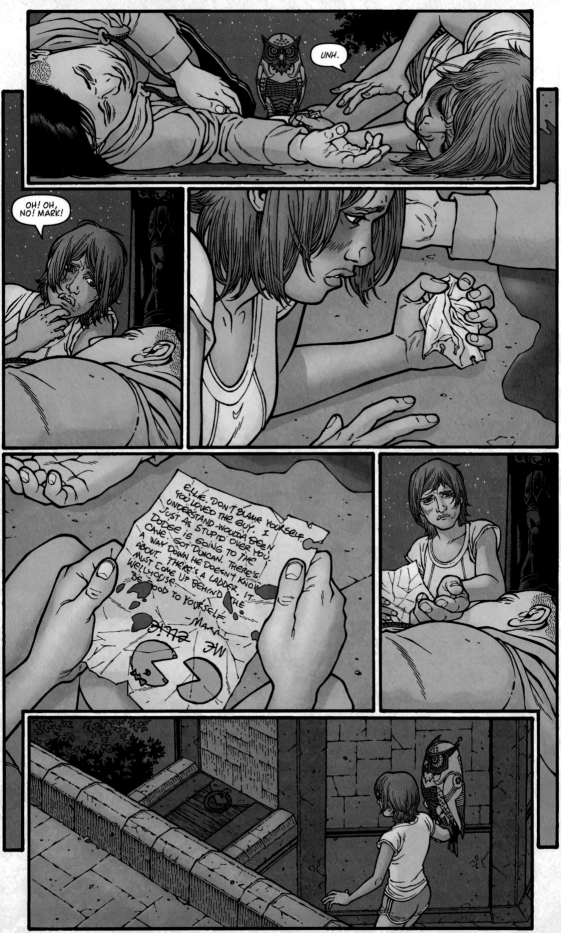

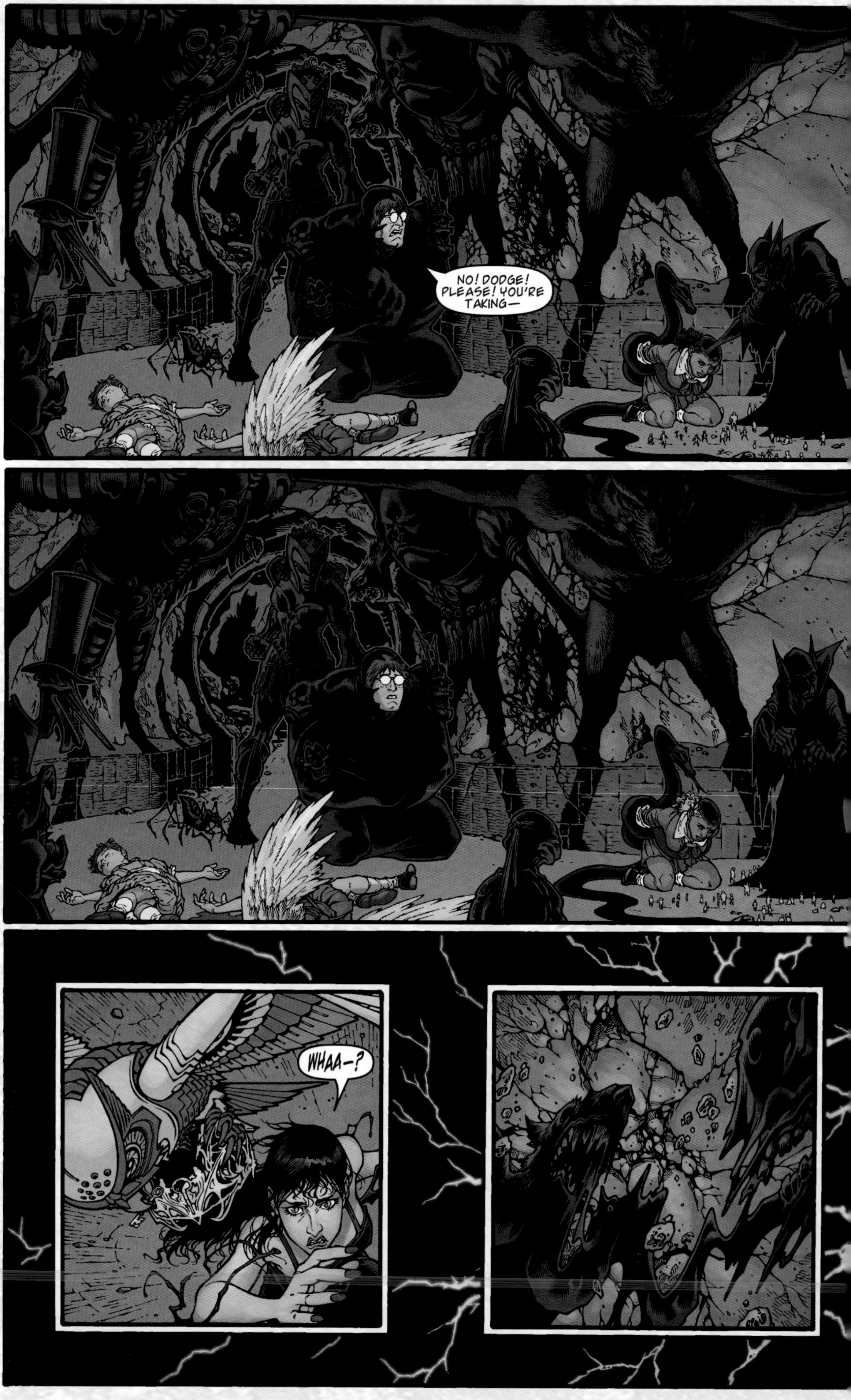
NO! DODGE! PLEASE! YOU'RE TAKING—
WHAA-?

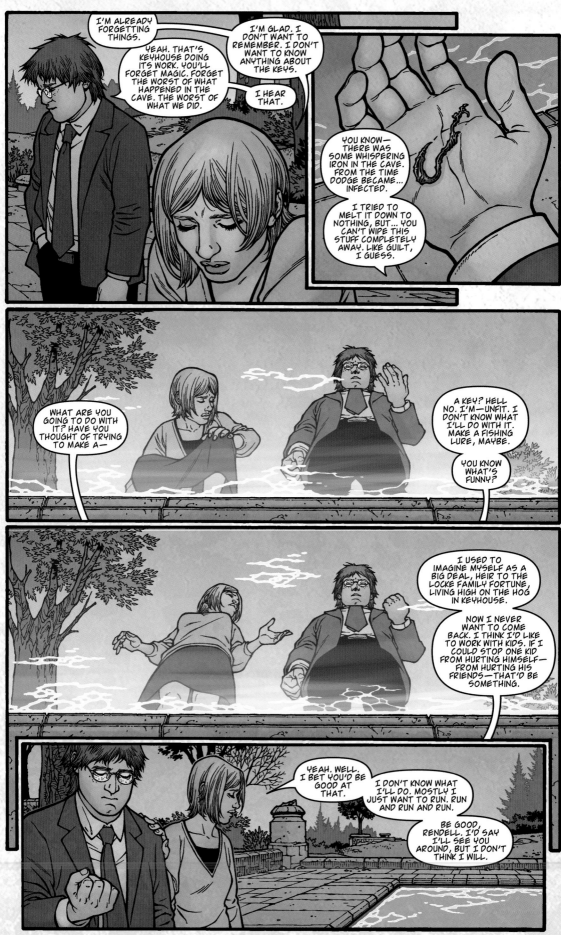

I'M ALREADY FORGETTING THINGS.

YEAH. THAT'S KEYHOUSE DOING ITS WORK. YOU'LL FORGET MAGIC. FORGET THE WORST OF WHAT HAPPENED IN THE CAVE. THE WORST OF WHAT WE DID.

I'M GLAD. I DON'T WANT TO REMEMBER. I DON'T WANT TO KNOW ANYTHING ABOUT THE KEYS.

I HEAR THAT.

YOU KNOW— THERE WAS SOME WHISPERING IRON IN THE CAVE. FROM THE TIME DODGE BECAME... INFECTED.

I TRIED TO MELT IT DOWN TO NOTHING, BUT... YOU CAN'T WIPE THIS STUFF COMPLETELY AWAY. LIKE GUILT, I GUESS.

WHAT ARE YOU GOING TO DO WITH IT? HAVE YOU THOUGHT OF TRYING TO MAKE A—

A KEY? HELL NO. I'M—UNFIT. I DON'T KNOW WHAT I'LL DO WITH IT. MAKE A FISHING LURE, MAYBE.

YOU KNOW WHAT'S FUNNY?

I USED TO IMAGINE MYSELF AS A BIG DEAL, HEIR TO THE LOCKE FAMILY FORTUNE, LIVING HIGH ON THE HOG IN KEYHOUSE.

NOW I NEVER WANT TO COME BACK. I THINK I'D LIKE TO WORK WITH KIDS. IF I COULD STOP ONE KID FROM HURTING HIMSELF— FROM HURTING HIS FRIENDS—THAT'D BE SOMETHING.

YEAH. WELL. I BET YOU'D BE GOOD AT THAT.

I DON'T KNOW WHAT I'LL DO. MOSTLY I JUST WANT TO RUN. RUN AND RUN AND RUN.

BE GOOD, RENDELL. I'D SAY I'LL SEE YOU AROUND, BUT I DON'T THINK I WILL.

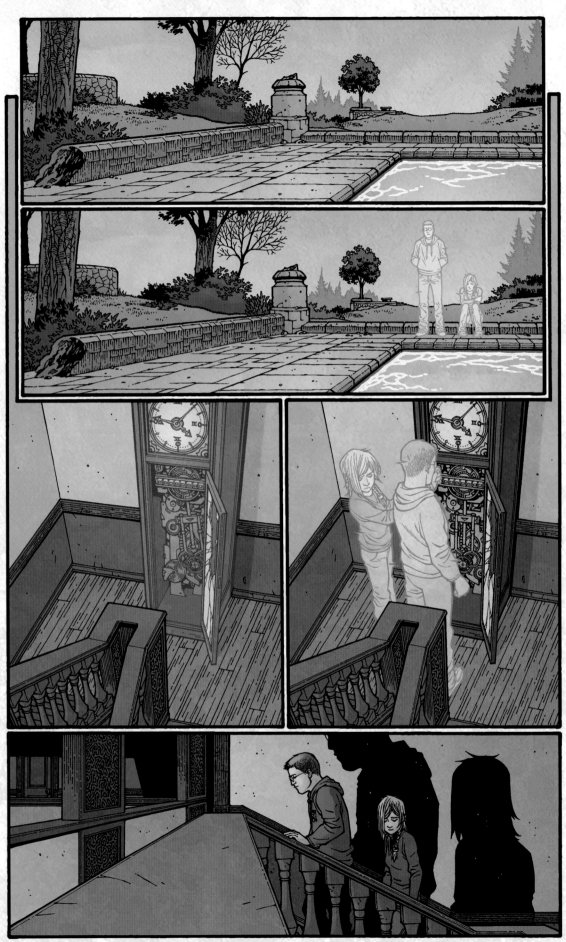

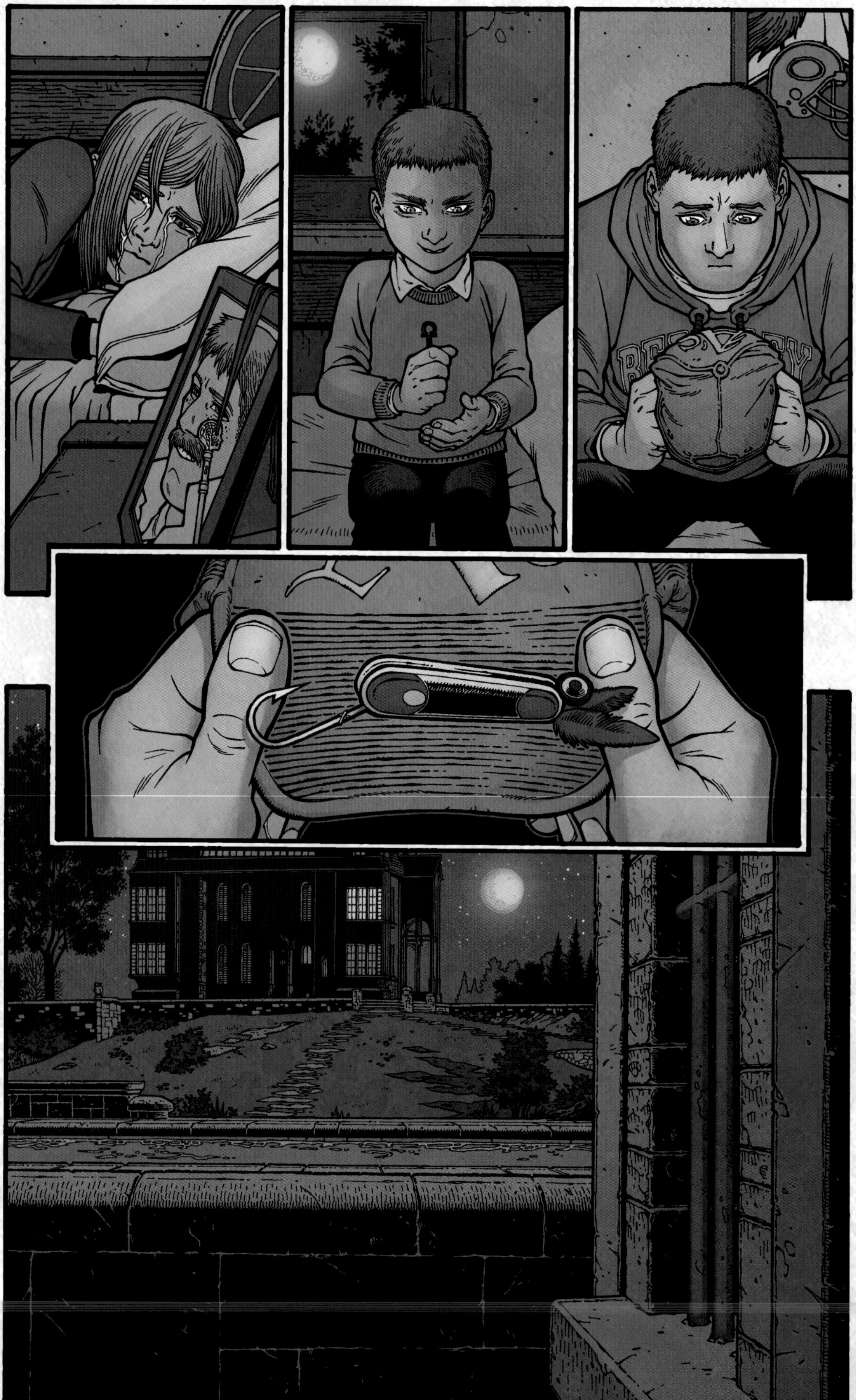

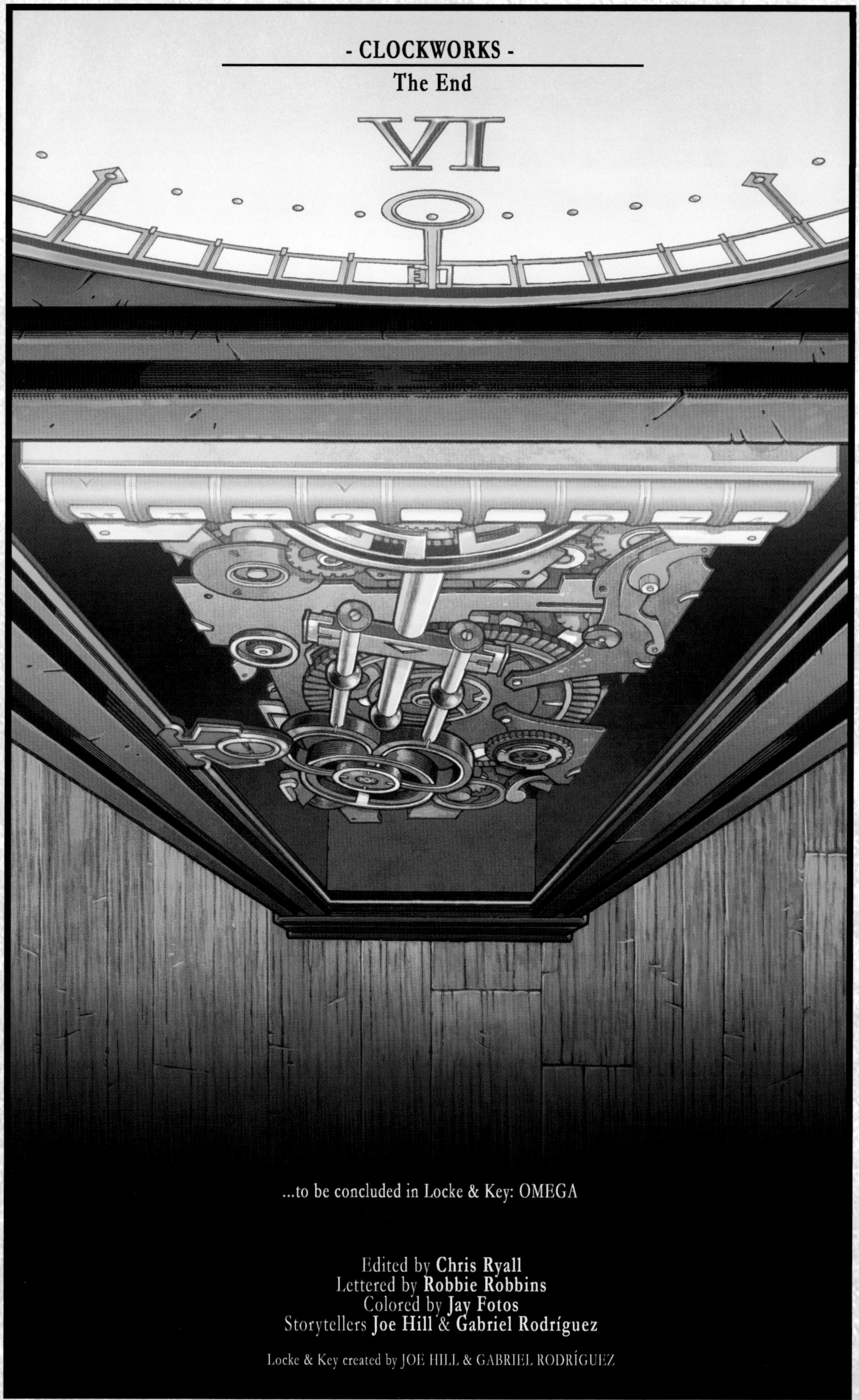
- CLOCKWORKS -
The End
VI
...to be concluded in Locke & Key: OMEGA
Edited by Chris Ryall
Lettered by Robbie Robbins
Colored by Jay Fotos
Storytellers Joe Hill & Gabriel Rodríguez
Locke & Key created by JOE HILL & GABRIEL RODRÍGUEZ

ΩΜEGΑ KEY

[text partially burned/obscured]

...in our t...
& I resolve...an...
hazzarded such a lock wo...
long I work'd in a fever...
till finallie t'was cast...
oh how, I feer'd! Ka...
in the gathr'd d...
straiked ou...
held the don...
beig'd G...
Gone...
ho...

THE KNOWN KEYS
(EXCERPTS FROM THE DIARY OF
BENJAMIN PIERCE LOCKE, 1757 - 1799)

GHOST KEY

onlee in occaisonull daith do I find
peece now, for with the bode caste
aisyde, it is possibull for one to know
his own ETERNALL SOULE. My spairt
cannot leeve the grounds of Keyhowse,
but heyre I walke laik an aingel!
I aim everywhare and nowhare at once,
from the tall's towair, to the deepst
caves. It is hard to dreem thair could
be any dore more terryble or
wondairfulle than that wych dyvydes
deth from lyfe, yet my expairances
at the thraishold of the black dore
have teach'd me thair are worse
things than to dyye...

ECHO KEY

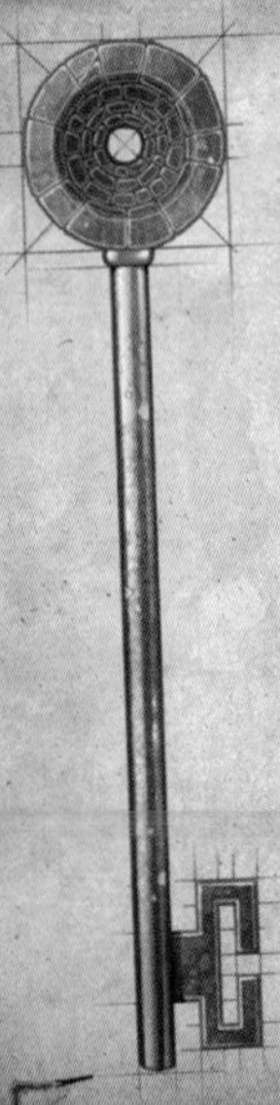

whence I unlock'd the dore I heerd a
voice that saimed to ecko from the
well & it aisk'd me who I sot & I spake
of my brother. No sooner had the
words pass'd my lips thence he ROSE from
the WELL like a spairt & yet was living
flaish, alltho he had dyed in the Drowning
Caves not 6 weeks beefor. He clasp'd me
to his bosom & sayd why do ye look so
unhappy to see me brother, but I wast
in feer for my allmaighty SOUL & fled
to the howse & pray'd thair to the
LORD
But in that grait howse, an ecko of
my voice was all the reeply I receiv'd

aNYWHeRe KeY

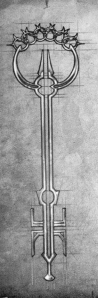

us'd the key to anyplaice againe, to return to Boston, & gaither intelaigents for Crais. 'Tis an act of terryble wychcraift, but better I do it, than my sister, who is obssaissed with REVENGING herself upon the RED-COATS, for thair violence agin our faither & brother & belov'd maither: Aye, my dredd of beeing called to acconnt someday by SATAN HIMSELF is a trifling concern when maiched with my desyre to rid the worlde of the devylls who taik the King's Coyne to do raip & murdur...

HeaD KeY

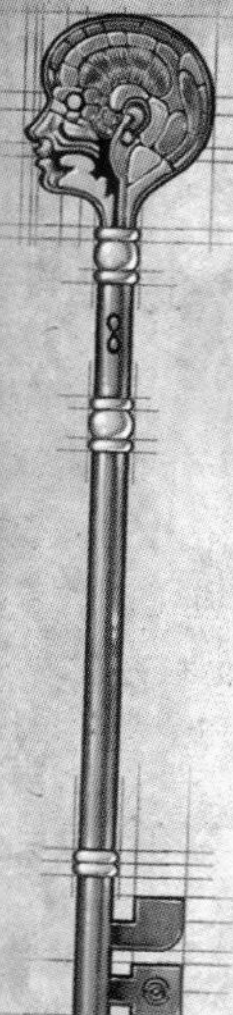

of alle the keys I have forged from the WHISP'RING IRON, 'tis the key that opens the human mind I most regrait. Miranda hast a pervairse fasinaytion whist the key & hast us'd ait to fill her head with all thair is to know about WAR & the SLAIYING of MEN, & she carrys an arsanall whist her whairever she goes. Yet I am less in dred of what she has put in than what she hast remov'd. Sometimes it is as if she is now without FEER and indeed is herself more man than I!

GeNDeR KeY

my sister - or should I now say my brother! - fights the shadow war with Crais in the streets of Boston whilst I wait at home, like a helpless maiden, praying to the ALLMAIGHTY! for her safe return. When first I fashin'd the key, I imaguined she maight trainsform to a boy to protect her, if necessaire, from the unsavorie lusts of ENGLISHMEN should the King's foot-soldiers return to Lovecraft to abuse God fairing womain. Never did I think she wouldst WILLENGLY caist off the wardrobe of her femininitie for this ruggaid liberation among men...

SHaDoW KeY

O Wycked Night! Damn'd be Crais & Damn'd be the Redcoats & Damn'd be my own foole self. Miranda tis griev'sly hurt & lingers on the thraishold of deth! The Redcoats pursued her & the tattr'd reminante of Crais's companie into the caves but I drove them back with the aide of the lyving shadows. If she dies I wouldst rather be a shadow myself than remain in thys diabollicall world, knowing she wouldst never have been at riske if not for me!

GiaNT KeY

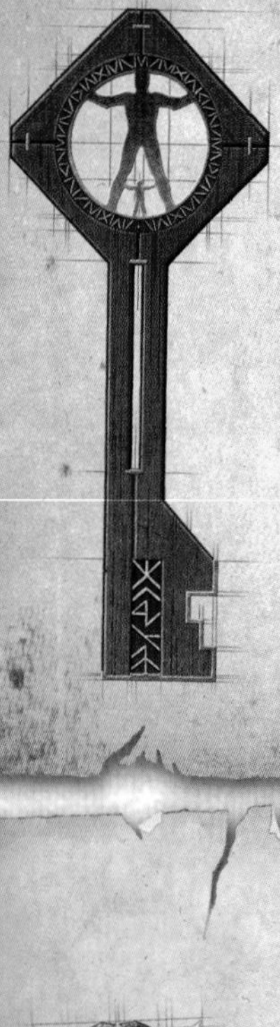

she is dying & thair is nothing I can do to save her!
The Redcoats return'd to assalle the house & claym her & I admitte I lette my fury & miserie get the better of me. I used the giant's key to multiplie my syze, so that my body was as vaste as my hayte & I turn'd upon a wholle regiment & ~ O GOD forgive me! ~ did detestably murther them alle!

MeNDiNG KeY

the Iron whispr'd to me laste night & I work'd in a fever alle day, mayking a cabinet & forging a new key out of that dreadfull metal that is not metal. Yet if the devil may pervairt Holie Scripture to serve his purposes, so may the rihteous at times turn the DEVILLS TOOLS to do the work of SWEET JESU! For the key & cabinet I fashin'd could be used to mend fraicturd objykts ~ shatter'd plattes, crack'd eggs & broken sistairs. Bless'd be THE LORD, Miranda hast recovr'd! I only wish she wouldst remembair her place & become the demure & modestte girlle she once was, but fear her love for Crais will emperille her againe soon enough...

Animal Key

September 9th, 1851~

...Ulysses said he would fly all the way to Hell if he had to, to find Delacorte for me. Clint said he would probably only be required to fly to Georgia, but that the two places were much alike, except Georgia is a bit hotter. We have fought a thousand times, my brothers and I, but this morning I felt I could not love any living souls more. Ulysses stepped through the door, and emerged on the other side, a golden eagle. He gave me a short, lordly look, and took to the skies...

Music Box Key

November 3rd, 1851~

...he was dying fast from his injuries and knew it. He said he would go to glory and take his secrets with him. Ulysses said that if our Lord meant to open the Gates Of Heaven to a B---- like him, he would prefer to throw in with the Devil. Clint hissed and seemed ready to strike again, but I restrained him. I knew if Hammersmith died, I would likely never see Delacorte again, and so I turned the Key in the Music Box, and the tune began to play. A miniature version of myself turned around and around, and sang:

 ...tell us who paid you for the girl...
 ...do it now before you leave this world...
Hammersmith's eyes widened, and he began to speak...

Skin Key

November 5th, 1851~

...I looked into the mirror, and turned it, so I became of the African race, and my skin was dark as coal. And it is a wonderment to me. All my thoughts had, until then, been bent on finding Delacorte and beseeching her to become free and white like myself. But when I saw my black features in the mirror, I was surprised to find I liked my own face better than I had ever liked it before. Ulysses considered me for the longest of times, before offering me my hat and saying, "Remember to keep your eyes down, Harland. You have the White Man's habit of meeting another man's gaze, but you will fare poorly if you behave that way here in Georgia."

EXCERPTS FROM *JOURNALS, SONNETS, THEORIES & NATURAL OBSERVATIONS, BOOK XVI*,
BY CHAMBERLIN MORSE WALTON LOCKE, DATED 1914

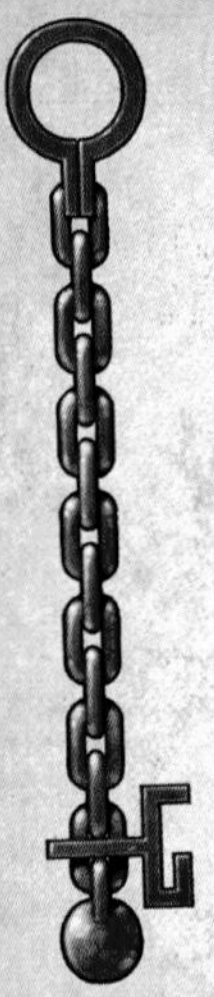

CHAIN KEY & THE GREAT LOCK

Something troublesome has happened. The Brougham Boys broke into the house this Sunday morning, while we were at church, and while attempting to enter the catacombs, triggered the Great Lock. I sorted them out with the Head Key, but I fear this is only the prelude to some new threat. The damnable thing is that they were sent with orders to break into the wine cellar, although they had no idea what they would find when they forced their way in. Someone must have some idea what I keep there, though, and someone is after it…

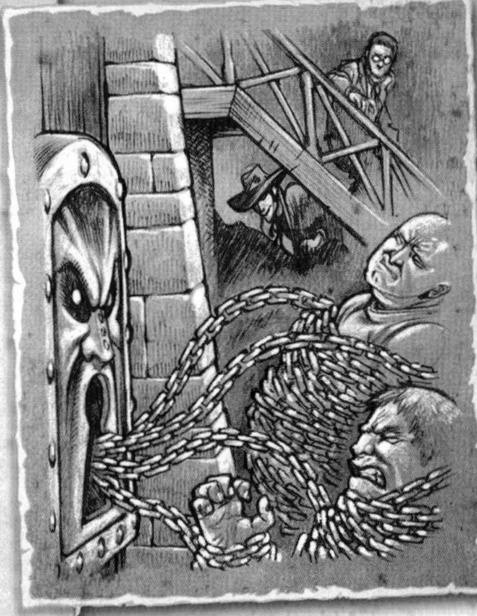

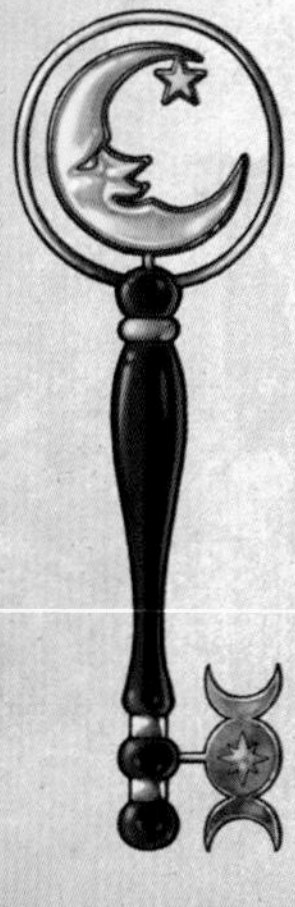

THE KEY TO THE MOON

There is nothing left to be done for little Ian. By the time the last fall apples are picked, his life will be wrenched from him in the most agonizing fashion, and no operation or final treatment will do anything to stop it from happening. Yet I think he hardly minds the pain that racks him nightly; nor has he any great terror of death. My brave boy! What he cannot bear is his own knowledge of all the vistas he will never see, all the people he will never meet, all the grand deeds he will never witness. It sickens me as well. I have asked Harland if he can fashion a key that can open a door in reality, a space between this life and the next. I am imagining a kind of balcony, high above the humorous tragedies and sad comedies of this earth, a place beyond pain, where the dead may gather to enjoy the great show of life below.

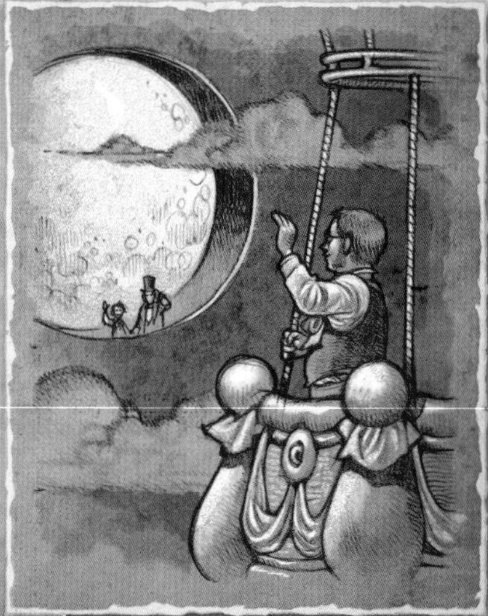

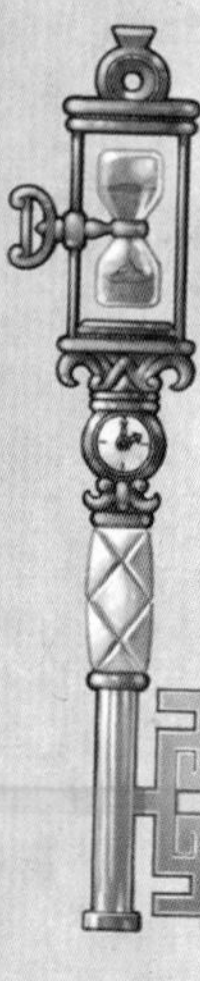

TIMESHIFT KEY

…Occasionally people will ask me about Ian, wanting to know how I am managing without him. I tell them honestly that I see him everyday, that he is with me always, here in this house. This usually earns me a consoling, worried look, but it is the perfect truth. With the aid of Harland's ingenious Timeshift Key and Clock, I am able to revisit all of the best days of Ian's life, as I wish. Of course I may also return Ian to our world with the Echo Key… but a human soul that has had its time on our earth longs for the warmth and comfort of That Other Place, and I know that bringing him back is something I would be doing for me, not for him. So I leave him be. I wonder, sometimes, what would happen if a truly twisted soul were to be reanimated with the Echo Key – someone with designs on the world of the living. Fortunately, I safeguard that key too closely for…

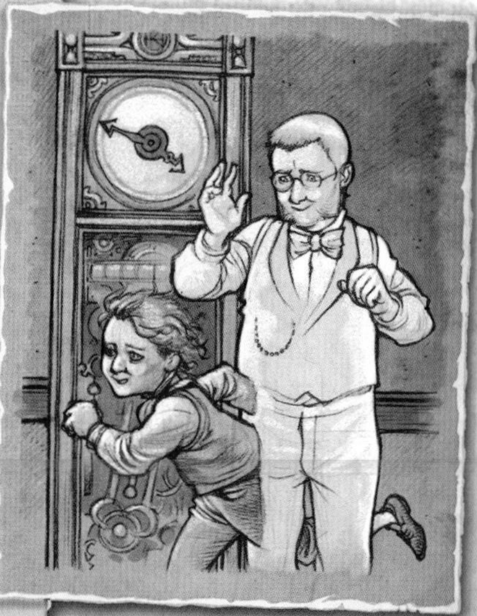

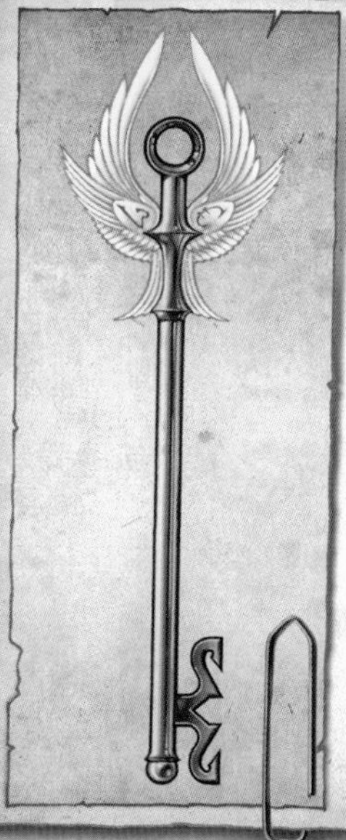

Engels-Schlüssel

4. Juni 1942

Mein Gott. Mein Gott! Bei Tagesanbruch war ich draußen und suchte nach dem kleinen Joe. Es stürmte und regnete in Strömen. Alles kam mir krank und unwirklich vor – wie in einem Albtraum. Ich rannte und rannte, völlig verzweifelt, und es war mir scheißegal, was er Jean über mich erzählte. Wenn er tot war, wollte ich selbst auch sterben. Und dann sah ich etwas Unglaubliches – etwas, das es gar nicht hätte geben dürfen, und ich bekam vor Überraschung und Staunen ganz weiche Knie. Ich sah Jean durch den Regen hinauffliegen, den zerschlagenen Körper ihres Bruders in der Armen. Sie trug das Gurtzeug mit den Flügeln, und hintendrin steckte der Schlüssel. Ich schwöre, sie ist geflogen! Und dabei sah sie so wunderschön aus wie eine Trauertaube.

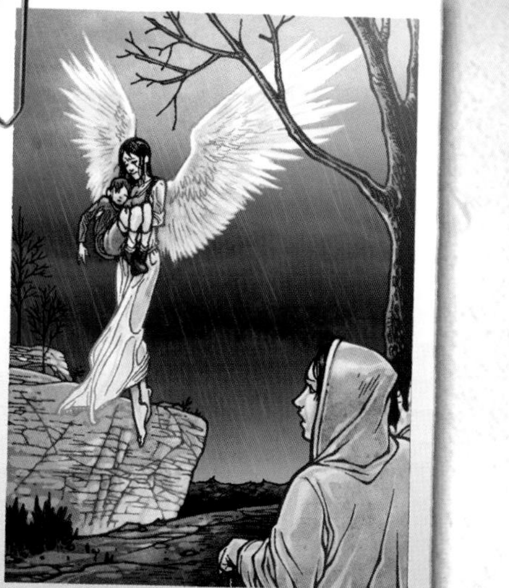

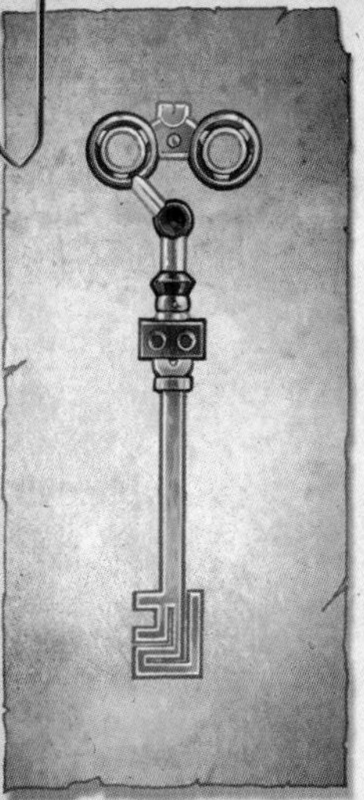

Philosophoscope Key

July 3rd, 1942

...Hannes asked me to come with him, in his quiet inflected English. I told him I liked it better when I thought he was mute because at least then he couldn't tell me lies. But I took his hand and went with him. He walked me to the Philosophoscope in the tower. Once I realized where we were going, Johnnie, I didn't want to go, and couldn't help myself. Once I realized what he was going to show me. He put the Key in, and shifted the lever to Truest Love and asked me to look. Oh Johnnie. How I have lied to myself for months. He knew what I would see somehow even when I didn't... that I would see him...

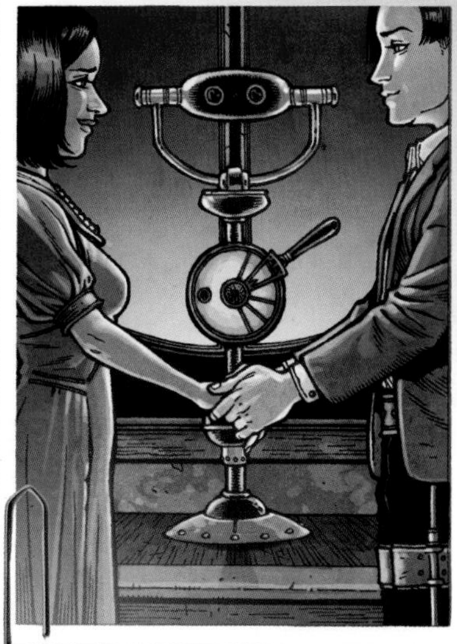

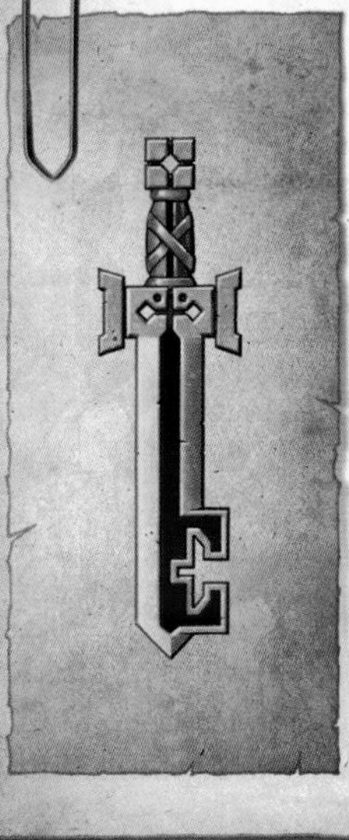

Herkules-Schlüssel

13. Juli 1942

Die Hälfte der 8. Armee und ein schier endloser Haufen SS-Männer warteten da auf mich! Ich schleuderte Eric gegen die Mauer und hörte, wie seine Rippen brachen, als wäre jemand auf ein Bündel Zweige gesprungen. Ich muss zugeben, das hörte sich wie Musik in meinen Ohren an!
Mit der anderen Hand schlug ich nach den Soldaten, und sie flogen wie Streichhölzer durch die Luft. Der Herkules-Schlüssel setzte all die Kraft in mir frei, die ich als verdammter Krüppel nie gehabt hatte. Aber der Sturmbannführer wusste, wie er mich fertigmachen konnte!

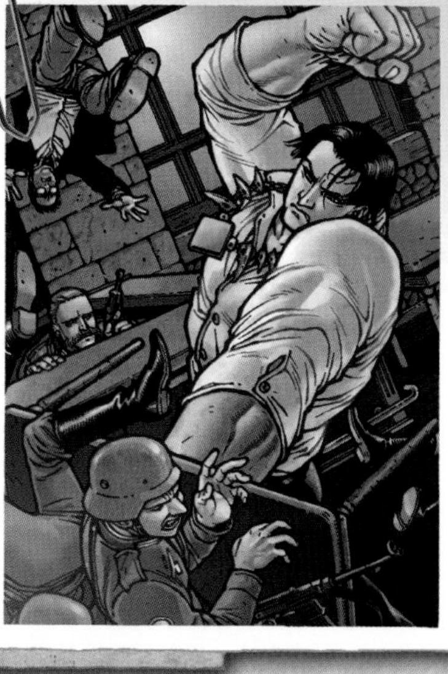

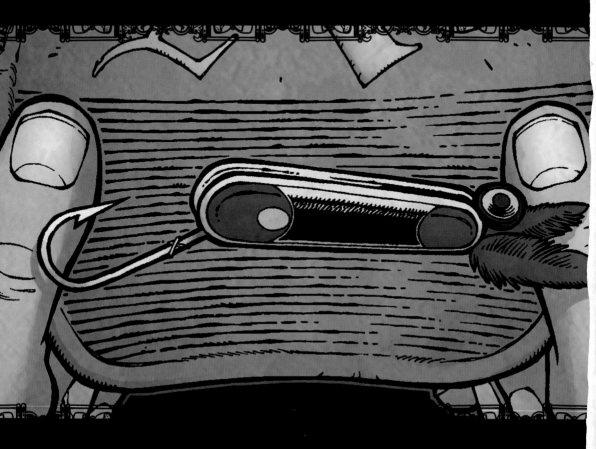

B I O G R A P H I E S

Joe Hill's first professional fiction submission was a SPIDER-MAN script, which he sent to Marvel Comics in 1984, at the age of twelve years old. It was turned down, but Joe received a handwritten note from then editor-in-chief Jim Shooter. It was impossible to read. He likes to believe it said, "You rock, kid! This is talent, baby!" Although it is possible the note actually said, "You rot, kid! This is toilet paper!" Twenty years later, Joe Hill sold his first comic script... an eleven-page story for *Spider-Man Unlimited*. Shortly after saw the publication of his first novel, the *New York Times* best-selling HEART-SHAPED BOX. He is also the author of HORNS and a book of stories, 20th CENTURY GHOSTS. He's won some prizes, most recently the 2011 Eisner Award for Best Writer. Hill and his separated-at-birth twin Gabriel Rodriguez have been working on the award-winning ongoing supernatural saga, LOCKE & KEY, since 2007.

Try to keep up with his active Twitter stream: @joe_hill

Gabriel Rodriguez was born in Santiago in 1974. He is a Chilean architect, and long-time comic-book lover, whose life took an unbelievable turn when, in 2002, he got the chance to collaborate for the first time with IDW Publishing. Breaking in to the comics industry with *CSI* and soon working on *Clive Barker's The Great and Secret Show*, *Beowulf*, and *George A. Romero's Land of the Dead*, in 2007 Rodriguez met Joe Hill and the two bonded like brothers. Together, they created the twisted but wonderful world of LOCKE & KEY. Rodriguez currently lives in Chile with his lovely wife Catalina and their wonderful children.

Follow his antics on Twitter: @GR_comics

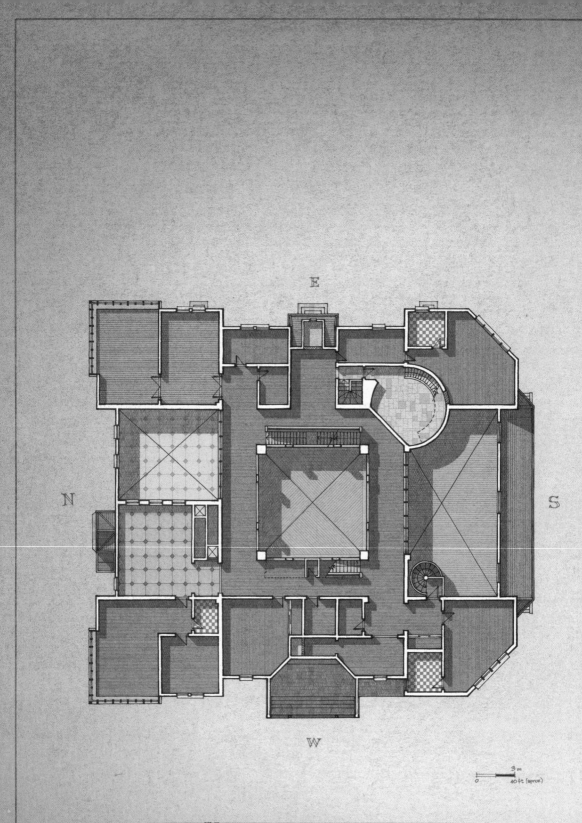

N

E

S

W

3 m

0

10 ft (aprox)

KEYHOUSE SECOND LEVEL